HOW TO STOP BEING A NARCISSIST

RECOGNIZE NARCISSISTIC BEHAVIORS, STOP BEING TOXIC, AND BUILD STRONG HEALTHY RELATIONSHIPS

MAX REED

Copyright© 2024 – Max Reed- All rights reserved.

The content contained within this book may not be reproduced, duplicated or transmitted without direct written permission from the author or the publisher.

Under no circumstances will any blame or legal responsibility be held against the publisher, or author, for any damages, reparation, or monetary loss due to the information contained within this book. Either directly or indirectly.

Legal Notice:

This book is copyright protected. This book is only for personal use. You cannot amend, distribute, sell, use, quote or paraphrase any part, or the content within this book, without the consent of the author or publisher.

Disclaimer Notice:

Please note the information contained within this document is for educational and entertainment purposes only. All effort has been executed to present accurate, up to date, and reliable, complete information. No warranties of any kind are declared or implied. Readers acknowledge that the author is not engaging in the rendering of legal, financial, medical or professional advice. The content within this book has been derived from various sources. Please consult a licensed professional before attempting any techniques outlined in this book.

By reading this document, the reader agrees that under no circumstances is the author responsible for any losses, direct or indirect, which are incurred as a result of the use of information contained within this document, including, but not limited to, — errors, omissions, or inaccuracies.

This book is intended for informational purposes only and is not a substitute for professional advice, diagnosis, or treatment. The content provided herein is designed to offer insights, share experiences, and present strategies related to personal development and overcoming narcissistic behaviors. It is important to acknowledge the complexity of such topics and the uniqueness of each individual's journey.

We strongly encourage readers to seek the guidance of qualified professionals for personalized advice and support. This book should not be used as the sole resource for making significant changes to your mental health or interpersonal relationships. Professional assistance is crucial in addressing complex personality traits and mental health issues, including narcissism.

While this book aims to increase your knowledge on the subject, it represents only a single source of information. Readers are advised to consult a variety of resources to gain a more comprehensive understanding of narcissism and related topics. Diversifying your sources of information will enhance your learning and provide a broader perspective on the subject matter.

It is essential to recognize that this book provides basic information and an introduction to the topics discussed. For those seeking deeper or more detailed insights, further research and exploration in the field are recommended. Do not rely solely on this book for all information regarding personal development and overcoming narcissistic traits.

Furthermore, it is important to manage expectations regarding the outcomes of reading this book. While it is designed to serve as a starting point on your journey toward self-improvement, it is not guaranteed to transform your life magically. The value of this book is commensurate with the investment made in purchasing it, and significant personal growth typically requires a commitment to continuous learning and exploration beyond this initial step.

In summary, treat this book as a tool to initiate your journey toward self-awareness and personal growth. It is a stepping stone towards a more profound exploration of yourself and your relationships with others. Remember, the path to improvement is ongoing and often requires resources beyond a single book. Engage actively in your journey, seek professional guidance, and remain open to learning from multiple sources to achieve the best outcomes on your path to transformation.

We're sorry if you come across any editing errors in the book. Please report them to bookbay.ct@gmail.com and any new ideas to improve the structure and information in the book.

Please, include the title of the book in the email object.

Thank you for your time and for being so cooperative with my team and me.

CONTENTS

Introduction	vi
1. UNVEILING NARCISSISM	1
What Defines Narcissism?	1
Origins of Narcissism	2
Self-Reflection: Identifying Narcissism Within	4
2. CULTIVATING SELF-AWARENESS	6
Daily Practices to Grow Your Empathy Muscle	7
Recognizing When and How to Apologize Sincerely	9
Building Emotional Intelligence	13
SMART Goals	16
Distinguishing Between NPD and Other Conditions	17
Healing the Inner Child	23
3. YOUR INNER CHILD	31
Recognizing Your Inner Child	34
The Impact of a Wounded Inner Child on Narcissistic Behavior	38
Healing Your Inner Child	43
Creative Expression and Play	48
4. ADDRESSING CORE NARCISSISTIC BEHAVIORS	52
Breaking the Narcissistic Cycle	52
Managing Anger and Control	56
Releasing the Need for Control	58
Approaches to Conflict Resolution	60
5. REINFORCING SELF-WORTH AND EMPATHY	62
Differentiating Narcissistic from Healthy Self-Esteem	62
Empathy as a Pathway to Change	67
Sustaining Personal Growth	70

6. ENHANCING INTERPERSONAL RELATIONSHIPS	74
Shifting Focus to Others	74
Empathetic Communication	80
Setting Healthy Boundaries	85
7. ADVANCED STRATEGIES FOR PERSONAL DEVELOPMENT	90
Mastering Emotional Regulation	90
Overcoming Compulsive Behaviors	94
Enhancing Relationship Dynamics	97
8. RELAPSE PREVENTION AND CONTINUOUS IMPROVEMENT	103
Identifying Signs of Relapse	103
Conclusion and Reflections	106
Free Gift For My Readers	108
Bonus: The Power of Mindfulness and Meditation	109
Keeping the Journey Going	113
Author's Note	114
References	115

INTRODUCTION

"Every step towards change is a step towards a better you." Max R.

Have you ever noticed your relationships starting strong but eventually falling apart, leaving you wondering what went wrong? Maybe friends have distanced themselves, or romantic partners have drifted away, and you're left feeling isolated and misunderstood. If you've ever questioned why your relationships don't last, it might be time to look inward. Narcissistic behaviors can create a barrier between you and the meaningful connections you crave.

This book is your lifeline out of that isolating cycle. It's not just about recognizing narcissistic behaviors; it's about transforming them into empathy, self-awareness, and healthy relationships. Together, we're going to untangle the web of narcissism, replace harmful patterns with genuine connection, and empower you to build a life filled with meaningful relationships.

Now, why take my word for it? Picture a younger me, oblivious to the impact of my actions, until one day, my partner confronted me about my behavior. She told me how my constant need for attention and lack of empathy were driving a wedge between us. That painful conversation was my wake-up call. It sparked a relentless pursuit to understand and change my narcissistic tendencies. It's been a journey filled with tough lessons, moments of clarity, and countless efforts to rebuild our relationship. Now, I'm here to share what I've learned with you.

This isn't your typical self-help book filled with jargon and impossible-to-follow advice. Think of it as your personal guide, crafted from real-life experiences, research, and practical strategies. We'll break down the complexities of narcissism into digestible, actionable steps. From understanding the root causes of your behavior to developing empathy and setting healthy boundaries, we've got you covered.

Here's a sneak peek: We'll start by defining what narcissism really is, helping you recognize its presence in your life. Next, we'll dive into cultivating self-awareness and empathy, followed by managing anger and control issues. You'll learn to set boundaries, improve your relationships, and sustain personal growth. Each chapter includes exercises and tools designed to make these changes stick.

I know you might be thinking, "Can I really change?" or "Is it worth the effort?" Trust me, the solutions in this book are practical and achievable. However, it's important to understand that this transformation won't happen overnight. Real, lasting change takes time, effort, and patience. But with persistence and dedication, you can make significant strides.

So, are you ready to start your journey towards a more empathetic and self-aware you? Let's do this together. Remember, you have the power to transform your behavior and improve your relationships.

We're in this together, supporting each other every step of the way. Welcome to "How to Stop Being a Narcissist: Recognize Narcissistic Behaviors, Stop Being Toxic, and Build Strong Healthy Relationships." Let the transformation begin.

CHAPTER 1
UNVEILING NARCISSISM

Understanding yourself is the first step to changing yourself.

WHAT DEFINES NARCISSISM?

Narcissism seems to be a hot topic these days, and it's more than just a buzzword. It's a term that gets thrown around a lot, often used to describe someone who's full of themselves or just plain vain. But let's dig a bit deeper because narcissism is more than just having a big ego. It's a way of thinking and acting that can hurt both the person who has it and those around them.

Narcissism is about having an inflated sense of self-importance, always craving praise, and not really caring about others' feelings. It's not just about loving yourself too much. Instead, it's about seeing yourself in an exaggerated way, focusing only on your own needs and wants while ignoring others.

If you picked up this book, maybe you suspect you might have some narcissistic traits. So, why do some folks end up being narcissists? Well, it often kicks off in childhood. If a kid's emotional needs are either overly met or completely ignored, they might grow up feeling insecure. And to hide this insecurity, they might act all superior and arrogant. So, a narcissist isn't just someone who's selfish; they're often covering up deep hurts and fears. Makes sense, right?

Now, just because you understand why you might be a narcissist doesn't mean you should excuse bad behavior. Narcissists can be manipulative and hurt others emotionally. You might always need to be admired, and this can turn your relationships toxic. The feelings and needs of others often get overlooked. It's a rough deal for everyone involved.

Here's a kicker – narcissism isn't the same for everyone. It's on a spectrum. On one end, you've got healthy narcissism, where a person has good self-esteem. But on the other end, there's malignant narcissism, which is seriously harmful and includes manipulative and aggressive behavior. Most folks are somewhere in between, showing narcissistic traits in different degrees.

Why should you care about this spectrum? Understanding that everyone has some narcissistic traits can help you spot and change your own behaviors. It helps you move away from harmful patterns and towards healthier relationships.

In a nutshell, narcissism isn't just about thinking you're awesome. It's a mix of insecurity, lack of empathy, and an exaggerated self-image. This way of thinking can hurt both you and those around you. But hey, with understanding and self-awareness, change is possible. The first step to stopping being a narcissist is understanding what narcissism really is. Stick with me, and you'll dig into the tools and strategies to help you make those changes.

ORIGINS OF NARCISSISM

Narcissism isn't just about being vain or self-absorbed; it's more complex and runs deeper than you might think. Various factors influence narcissistic behavior. Often, narcissism develops as a way to cope with deep insecurities and fears. Many people with narcissistic traits have fragile self-esteem. Ever feel like your confidence is just a mask? Acting superior can be a way to protect yourself from feeling inadequate or rejected.

Did you know that genetics and brain biology also play a role in narcissism? Research shows that people with narcissistic traits have different brain structures and functions related to empathy and emotional control. This biological factor, combined with life experiences, can lead to narcissistic behavior. On the other hand, our society also affects how narcissism develops. We often value individual success and perfection, pushing people to focus too much on their own achievements and image. Do you feel pressure to be perfect or to always succeed?

Narcissism can also be a way to avoid dealing with emotional pain or trauma. By focusing on your own needs, you might ignore hurtful memories. Have you ever used your behavior to escape from painful feelings? It's easy to think of narcissists as just selfish people, but understanding the reasons behind their behavior helps you see them differently. It's not about excusing actions but understanding what drives them. This is important in your journey to stop being narcissistic.

Narcissism isn't something you are born with; it's learned from a mix of genetics, environment, and society. Understanding this is the first step to change. It's about seeing beyond the surface and recognizing the deep fears and insecurities that cause narcissistic behavior.

In the end, it's not about blaming yourself or others for being narcissistic. It's about recognizing these traits, understanding their roots, and taking steps to change. It's about freeing yourself from narcissism and living a more genuine and caring life. Knowing the causes of narcissism is not the end goal; it's a step towards a life free from these traits.

The Spectrum of Narcissism: It's Not All the Same

You might think all narcissists are cut from the same cloth, but that's not the case. Narcissism shows up differently in different people. Understanding this can help you see where you fit and how you can change.

At one end of the spectrum is healthy narcissism. I know, it sounds strange, but a little bit of narcissism is actually good for you. It helps you feel confident and achieve your goals. This type of narcissism boosts your self-esteem without making you lose empathy for others. But as you move further along the spectrum, narcissism becomes less healthy. Do you always need praise and feel more important than others? This could be a sign of too much narcissism, which can harm your relationships and life. When narcissism becomes extreme, it's called Narcissistic Personality Disorder (NPD). This is when narcissism causes serious problems in how someone acts and feels. Even within NPD, people can show different levels of these traits. Some might have strong narcissistic behaviors but don't fully meet the criteria for NPD. Others might have all the symptoms, making it very hard for them to have healthy relationships or function well in life.

Narcissism also shows up in two main types: overt and covert. Have you met someone who always boasts and seeks attention? That's overt narcissism. These people seem confident and superior but don't care how their actions affect others. On the other hand, covert narcissists are harder to spot. They hide their sense of superiority behind fake humility or by playing the victim. They manipulate others subtly, often making you feel sorry for them.

Why is it important to know where you stand on this spectrum? Because it helps you understand yourself better and start making changes. It takes courage to admit you have narcissistic traits, but this honesty is the first step to improvement. Narcissism can be a big challenge, but remember, you can change. By becoming aware of your behaviors, committing to personal growth, and getting the right support, you can balance your self-perception. You can build real self-esteem, learn empathy, and have healthier, happier relationships.

SELF-REFLECTION: IDENTIFYING NARCISSISM WITHIN

"Change starts with seeing the truth about ourselves."

Do you ever wonder if you have narcissistic traits? If you picked up this book, you might be curious or even concerned. To change, you need to take a hard look at yourself. Self-reflection can reveal things you don't like, but seeing these things is the first step to becoming better.

Narcissism isn't always obvious. It can sneak up on you in small ways. Do you often need others to admire you? Do you find it hard to care about others' feelings? Do you feel like you deserve special treatment? These behaviors might be so familiar that you don't even notice them. But becoming aware of them is the first step to change.

One common sign of narcissism is always needing praise. Do you try hard to get others to approve of you, even if it makes you unhappy? Recognizing this can help you start finding self-worth inside yourself instead of looking for it from others. Another sign is a lack of empathy. Do you struggle to understand how others feel? Do you ignore their emotions because you're focused on your own needs? Seeing this in yourself can push you to start practicing empathy and caring more about others.

Feeling entitled is another narcissistic behavior. Do you think you should get special treatment or feel you're better than others? This can make you ignore what others need. Noticing this can help you start treating others with the respect they deserve.

Recognizing these behaviors isn't about beating yourself up. It's about becoming more aware. It's about understanding that no one is perfect and that you can always improve. It's about owning your flaws and trying to be better, not for others, but for yourself.

The journey to improve is also a journey to understand yourself. It's about looking inside and facing the truths you find there. It's about learning to love yourself, flaws and all. And it's about treating others with kindness and respect. Seeing narcissistic behaviors in yourself is just the start. The real work is in changing these behaviors. It's a tough journey, but it's worth it. In the end, you can only change yourself. So let's start this journey today. Let's become better versions of ourselves.

CHAPTER 2
CULTIVATING SELF-AWARENESS

True empathy is seeing the world through another's eyes

What does empathy really mean to you? I know it sounds like a heavy word, but it's really about understanding and sharing the feelings of others. It's like putting yourself in someone else's shoes and feeling their emotions as if they were your own. This is super important for forming meaningful and healthy relationships, but it can be challenging, especially if you have narcissistic tendencies. Empathy goes beyond just feeling sorry for someone. It's about truly absorbing their emotional state, seeing things from their perspective, and responding supportively. Do you often consider what others might be feeling? Recognizing that everyone has their own valid experiences and emotions is a big part of empathy.

Why is empathy so difficult? It requires vulnerability. You have to be willing to step out of your comfort zone, expose your emotions, and be affected by the emotions of others. For narcissists, who are often focused on their own feelings and needs, this can be very challenging. Do you find it hard to let down your guard and connect with others on an emotional level?

Narcissists struggle with empathy because they are usually consumed by their own desires and feelings. This self-focus can lead to negative behaviors like manipulation, exploitation, and emotional abuse. It can also create a lack of emotional intimacy, leaving you feeling lonely and isolated. Do you sometimes feel disconnected from those around you?

But here's the good news: narcissism isn't a life sentence. Empathy can be learned, and narcissistic tendencies can be unlearned. This requires self-awareness, self-reflection, and a willingness to change. Are you ready to acknowledge your narcissistic tendencies and make a conscious effort to focus more on others? Practicing empathy means regularly stepping outside of your own world. It's not just about feeling bad for someone; it's about understanding their experiences and responding with compassion. Do you recognize that other people's feelings matter just as much as your own?

Empathy is challenging, but not impossible. It's a skill that can be developed through practice and dedication. This journey will lead to more meaningful relationships, a greater sense of connection with others, and a deeper understanding of yourself and the world. Are you willing to take this journey?

To stop being a narcissist, start by understanding and cultivating empathy. I know, it's tough. Acknowledge your tendencies, understand the importance of empathy, and practice it regularly, even when it's tough. This journey is challenging, but the rewards are worth it. You'll build stronger relationships, feel more connected, and gain a better understanding of yourself and others.

DAILY PRACTICES TO GROW YOUR EMPATHY MUSCLE

Do you often find it hard to understand others' feelings? Growing empathy is like exercising a muscle; it takes daily practice. Here are some daily habits to help you develop empathy, which you might have been missing as a narcissist.

- **Active Listening:** Ever really tried to listen to someone, not just hear their words? Active listening means understanding their perspective and emotions, paying attention to non-verbal cues, and

responding in a way that shows you care about their thoughts and feelings. This is different from focusing on yourself, but with practice, it becomes natural and rewarding.
- **Cultivating Curiosity:** Do you often think more about yourself than others? Try to be curious about people's experiences, interests, and emotions. Ask someone about their day or their opinion on a topic, and genuinely listen to their response. This shifts your focus outward and helps build connections.
- **Practicing Mindfulness:** Are you aware of your thoughts and feelings in the moment? Mindfulness helps you understand your emotions and reactions, which can help you relate to others. It also helps you notice when you're falling back into narcissistic behaviors, allowing you to correct yourself.
- **Expressing Gratitude:** Do you often feel like the world owes you something? Try to express gratitude for the kindness and efforts of others. Thank someone for their help or keep a gratitude journal to note things you're grateful for each day. This can break down your sense of entitlement.
- **Validating Others' Emotions:** Do you struggle to acknowledge others' feelings? Even if you don't agree with them, making an effort to validate others' emotions helps build emotional intelligence and empathy. It's about recognizing that their feelings are just as important as yours.
- **Putting Yourself in Others' Shoes:** Do you try to imagine how others feel? Whenever you interact with someone, take a moment to consider their perspective. This classic empathy-building exercise is especially effective for overcoming narcissism.

Growing your empathy muscle takes time and patience. You may not see changes overnight, but with consistent practice, you'll notice a shift in your attitudes and behaviors. Stay committed to these daily practices, even when it feels challenging. Over time, these small changes can lead to a significant transformation, helping you to become a more empathetic and compassionate person.

RECOGNIZING WHEN AND HOW TO APOLOGIZE SINCERELY

Do you find it tough to say "I'm sorry" and really mean it? Apologizing sincerely is more than just uttering those words. It's about understanding the impact of your actions, taking responsibility, and showing a genuine commitment to change. If you've been avoiding blame or deflecting criticism, it's time to break that habit. I know it's not easy, but empathy is your key here. Have you ever tried to truly grasp how the other person feels? Putting yourself in their shoes helps you see the consequences of your actions from their viewpoint.

When someone tells you they're hurt or disappointed, do you actually listen? Instead of jumping to defend yourself, take in their words and emotions. Think about their feelings and imagine how you would feel in their place. This understanding helps you recognize when an apology is needed. But knowing when to apologize is just the start. Do you know how to apologize sincerely? A genuine apology goes beyond just saying the words. It's about truly meaning them.

First, take full responsibility for your actions. Admit that you were wrong without making excuses or blaming others. Focus on what you did and how it affected the other person, not on their reaction. Next, express genuine remorse. Show that you understand how the other person feels and that you regret causing them pain. Your tone and body language should reflect your sincerity. Finally, make a commitment to change. Show that you're willing to learn from your mistakes and avoid repeating them in the future.

Change takes time, and you might slip up, but what matters is your consistent effort to improve. Your apologies will become more sincere as you develop empathy and take responsibility for your actions. Sincere apologies can be challenging, especially if you have narcissistic tendencies. It requires a shift in mindset and a willingness to step out of your comfort zone. But it's a necessary step toward becoming less narcissistic. By learning to apologize sincerely, you improve your relationships and foster personal growth.

Apologizing sincerely is a step toward becoming more self-aware, compassionate, and less narcissistic. Each genuine apology is a step forward in your journey of change. Are you ready to make this commitment and build better relationships with others?

Exercises for Practicing Authentic Apologies

Do you find it hard to apologize sincerely? Authentic apologies can heal wounds, rebuild trust, and strengthen relationships. Here are some exercises to help you practice and master the art of genuine apologies.

- **Reflect on Past Mistakes**: Think of a time when you wronged someone but never apologized. It could be something small, like forgetting a friend's birthday, or something big, like breaking someone's trust. Write down what happened from the other person's perspective. How do you think they felt because of your actions? This helps build empathy.
- **Drafting an Apology**: Once you understand their feelings, write an apology. Focus on their feelings, not your own. Acknowledge the hurt you caused, express genuine regret, and offer to make things right. Avoid saying, "If you felt hurt" or "If I did something wrong." These phrases sound insincere. Instead, take full responsibility for your actions.
- **Role-Playing**: Find a friend or mentor to help you practice. Have them play the person you're apologizing to. Deliver your apology and listen to their feedback. This helps you see how your words and tone come across, ensuring your apology shows real remorse and empathy.
- **Practicing Humility**: Do you find it hard to admit when you're wrong? Set aside time each day to acknowledge your mistakes and

shortcomings. Write them in a journal or reflect on them quietly. This practice helps you become comfortable with imperfection and makes it easier to apologize sincerely.
- **Daily Apologies**: Make apologizing a habit in your daily life. Start with small things, like bumping into someone or interrupting them. This normalizes apologizing for you and makes it less intimidating when you need to make bigger apologies.

Remember, these exercises aren't about punishing yourself or dwelling on mistakes. They're about learning, growing, and becoming more empathetic. Be patient with yourself. Change takes time, and it's okay to stumble along the way. What matters is that you're making an effort to become a better person.

Learning to apologize sincerely is crucial in overcoming narcissism. It requires empathy, humility, and a willingness to take responsibility for your actions. Practicing these exercises regularly helps you develop these qualities and become more capable of offering sincere and meaningful apologies. Are you ready to start practicing and see the positive changes it brings?

DAILY JOURNALING PROMPTS

Integrating daily journaling into your routine offers a practical, introspective method for addressing narcissistic tendencies. Here's how you can make the most out of it, with concrete prompts to guide your journey toward self-awareness and empathy.

Step-by-Step Guide to Daily Journaling:

1. **Choose Your Medium**: Whether it's a traditional notebook or a digital app, pick what feels most comfortable for you.

2. Set a Daily Reminder: Consistency is key. Choose a time each day dedicated to journaling, even if it's just for five minutes.
3. Create a Safe Space: Your journal is a judgment-free zone. Be honest and open with your entries; this is for your eyes only.

Practical Journaling Prompts:

1. Today's Reflection: Start with a simple reflection on your day. What were the highs and lows? This helps in grounding your thoughts and emotions.
2. Self-Observation: "Today, I noticed I felt threatened when..." Describe the situation and explore why it triggered you. What does this say about your needs or insecurities?
3. Empathy Expansion: "A situation where I could have shown more empathy was..." Reflect on why empathy was lacking and how you could approach it differently next time.
4. Gratitude Moments: List three small things you were grateful for today. Gratitude shifts focus from self-centeredness to appreciation of the world around you.
5. Criticism and Growth: "A piece of criticism I received today was..." How did you react? Explore constructive ways to use this feedback for personal growth.
6. Understanding Reactions: "An instance where my reaction was stronger than expected was..." Delve into the emotions and thoughts behind this reaction. What might be a more balanced response?
7. Introspection on Control: "Today, I sought control over... because..." Understanding your need for control can reveal underlying fears or insecurities.
8. Navigating Conflicts: "A conflict I encountered today was..." Reflect on your role in the conflict and how empathy and understanding could alter the outcome.

9. Self-Praise: Identify one thing you did well today. Acknowledging your strengths builds a healthier self-image.
10. Future Steps: "One step I can take tomorrow to be less self-centered is..." Planning concrete actions for change keeps you focused on growth.

Tips for Effective Journaling:

- Be Consistent: Even on days when it feels challenging, stick to your journaling routine.
- Review Regularly: Look back on your entries every month. This will help you see patterns, recognize growth, and adjust your focus as needed.
- Combine with Therapy: If possible, use journaling in conjunction with therapy. It can provide valuable insights for discussions with your therapist.

Journaling is more than writing down your thoughts; it's an act of self-discovery and a step toward change. By using these prompts to examine your behaviors, thoughts, and emotions, you're laying the groundwork for genuine self-awareness and empathy. Remember, the journey is ongoing, and every entry is a step forward on your path to personal growth.

BUILDING EMOTIONAL INTELLIGENCE

Real change happens through daily habits

. . .

Have you ever thought about why some people seem to handle their emotions so well? They might have strong emotional intelligence. Building emotional intelligence means understanding your own emotions and those of others. It helps you make better decisions and form healthier relationships.

- **Self-Awareness**: Do you know how you feel at different times of the day? Being aware of your emotions is the first step. Take a moment each day to check in with yourself. Ask, "How am I feeling right now?" This helps you understand your emotional patterns and what triggers them.
- **Self-Regulation**: Have you ever reacted without thinking and regretted it later? Learning to control your reactions is crucial. When you feel a strong emotion, like anger or frustration, take a deep breath and count to ten. Ask yourself, "Is this the best way to respond?" This pause can prevent many problems and help you stay calm.
- **Motivation**: What drives you to get out of bed in the morning? Knowing what motivates you can help you stay focused and positive. Set small, achievable goals for yourself each day. When you accomplish them, you'll feel more motivated to keep going. Ask, "What do I want to achieve today?" This keeps you on track and gives you a sense of purpose.
- **Empathy**: Do you try to understand how others feel? Empathy is about putting yourself in someone else's shoes. When someone shares their feelings with you, listen carefully. Ask, "How would I feel in their situation?" This helps you connect with others and respond in a supportive way.
- **Social Skills**: Do you find it easy to talk to others and build relationships? Good social skills are part of emotional intelligence. Practice active listening and clear communication. When talking to someone, focus on what they're saying instead of thinking about your response. Ask, "Am I really listening to them?" This makes

your conversations more meaningful and helps build stronger connections.

Daily Practices:

1. **Morning Check-In**: Start your day by asking yourself how you feel. This sets the tone for your day and helps you be more aware of your emotions.
2. **Pause and Reflect**: When you feel a strong emotion, pause and think before reacting. Ask, "What's the best way to handle this?"
3. **Set Goals**: Write down one or two things you want to achieve each day. This keeps you motivated and focused.
4. **Practice Empathy**: When someone shares their feelings, listen and try to understand their perspective. Ask, "How would I feel in their shoes?
5. **Build Relationships**: Make an effort to connect with others. Practice listening and responding thoughtfully.

Improving emotional intelligence takes time and practice. Start with small steps and be patient with yourself. Notice the changes in how you understand and manage your emotions. Are you more aware of your feelings? Are your relationships getting better?

By working on your emotional intelligence every day, you can make a big difference in your life. It helps you become more aware of yourself and others, leading to better decisions and stronger relationships.

SMART GOALS

Have you thought about how setting goals can guide you toward self-improvement? Setting realistic goals and tracking your progress is crucial in overcoming narcissistic tendencies. This approach helps you stay focused and see how far you've come.

Realistic goals are important for making progress. Think about goals that challenge you but are still possible with effort. They should be *Specific, Measurable, Achievable, Relevant, and Time-bound* (SMART). For example, a goal like "I will listen and show empathy in my conversations at least once a day for the next month" is a SMART goal. It's clear, you can measure it, it's doable, it matters to your growth, and it has a deadline.

Why should you set goals? Goals give you something to aim for and a plan to follow. Each goal you reach is a step toward becoming less self-centered. Picture your goals as checkpoints that mark your progress on your journey. How do you know if you're moving forward? Tracking your progress shows you where you started, how much you've achieved, and what's left to do. It's not about feeling bad if you miss a goal. It's about learning and improving.

Recognizing your achievements, even small ones, is important because they show that you can change and are changing. Celebrating these milestones can motivate you to keep going, even when it's tough. Do you write down your thoughts? Keeping a journal helps you see your successes and areas for improvement. Have you tried using an app to track your goals? Many tools are designed to help you keep track of your progress. Reflecting on your progress can be as simple as taking a moment to think about what you've achieved.

Can you be truthful about your progress? Narcissism can make it hard to see yourself clearly. It's important to be honest. If you didn't meet a goal, don't ignore it. Understand why and use that knowledge to improve next time.

Are you aware of how your actions affect others? Spend time each day thinking about your interactions. Ask yourself, "How did I make others feel today?" This helps you understand and respect others' emotions and viewpoints. Do you try to understand others' feelings? Make it a habit to put yourself in their shoes. Listen carefully when they talk and show that you care. Over time, this will help you become more aware of others' emotions and needs, building stronger connections.

By setting realistic goals and tracking your progress, you can make significant strides in overcoming narcissism. Remember, the aim is not to be perfect but to be better than you were yesterday.

DISTINGUISHING BETWEEN NPD AND OTHER CONDITIONS

Have you ever wondered if what you're feeling is truly Narcissistic Personality Disorder (NPD) or something else? Knowing the difference is crucial because it helps you understand what's going on and find the best ways to improve. Sometimes, people mix up NPD with just being arrogant or self-centered. Do you know someone who seems full of themselves but doesn't have NPD? NPD goes deeper and affects daily life and relationships in a big way. People with NPD often feel very important and lack empathy, but these traits are so strong they cause serious problems.

Have you heard of Antisocial Personality Disorder (ASPD)? It's another condition that looks a bit like NPD. People with ASPD can also be manipulative and lack empathy. However, they often break the law and don't care about others' safety. In contrast, people with NPD might do similar things but usually because they crave admiration and attention, not because they want to break rules.

Then there's Borderline Personality Disorder (BPD). Both BPD and NPD can involve intense emotions and unstable relationships, but BPD is more about having moods and relationships that are all over the place, while NPD is about feeling superior and entitled. Do you sometimes feel like you're better than others or deserve special treatment?

Histrionic Personality Disorder (HPD) can also be confused with NPD. People with HPD are very dramatic and need to be the center of attention. They don't necessarily think they are better than others; they just want attention, whether it's good or bad. Does this sound like you, or do you seek admiration because you believe you're superior?

Understanding these differences is important. It's not about labeling yourself but about recognizing patterns in your behavior. This can help you figure out what you need to work on. If you see traits of NPD in yourself, talking to a mental health professional can provide a clear picture and help you find the right path to improvement.

Do you sometimes find it hard to see yourself clearly? Narcissism can distort self-perception. Being honest with yourself is key. If you notice behaviors that cause problems in your life or relationships, acknowledging them is the first step. Seeking help shows strength, not weakness. A professional can help you understand your behaviors and guide you on how to change them.

Compassion towards yourself is crucial. Recognizing and accepting flaws isn't failure; it's a brave move towards change. It's about peeling away the layers of narcissism to reveal your true self. Do you think you rely too much on others for validation? Learning to love and accept yourself can replace that need.

Focus Section: Differentiating NPD from Other Disorders

I know it's tough, but understanding the differences between NPD and other disorders is crucial. Narcissism isn't just arrogance; NPD affects your daily life and relationships big time. Traits like grandiosity and lack of empathy aren't just annoying—they cause real problems.

You've probably heard about Antisocial Personality Disorder (ASPD). People mix it up with NPD because both involve manipulation and lack of empathy. But folks with ASPD often break laws and don't care about rules because they disregard societal norms. Do you break rules just for kicks, or are you craving admiration and validation?

Then there's Borderline Personality Disorder (BPD). Sure, it shares intense emotions and unstable relationships with NPD, but BPD is all about mood swings and instability in self-image and relationships. NPD folks feel superior and entitled all the time. Do your relationships struggle because you're constantly seeking validation and recognition?

Histrionic Personality Disorder (HPD) is another one that gets confused with NPD. People with HPD love attention and are emotionally dramatic. They might seem self-centered, but they just want to be in the spotlight—not necessarily feel superior. Are you always craving attention, or is it more about seeking admiration and validation?

Understanding these differences helps you get a grip on your own behaviors and motivations. It's not easy to see these traits in yourself, but it's a crucial step towards self-awareness and growth. Professional help can provide clarity and guide you through these complex behaviors. Do you often feel misunderstood or misdiagnosed? Working with a mental health professional can give you a thorough assessment and tailored strategies to manage narcissistic traits.

Being honest about your progress is key. Narcissism can cloud your self-perception, but recognizing your behaviors and their impact is essential. Didn't meet a goal? Don't ignore it—figure out why and learn from it. Compassion for yourself is vital. Recognizing and accepting your flaws isn't failure; it's a brave move towards change. It's about peeling away layers of narcissism to reveal your true self. Do you think you rely too much on others for validation? Learning to love and accept yourself can replace that need.

By differentiating NPD from other disorders and seeking the right help, you can better understand your behaviors and make meaningful changes. This journey is deeply personal and involves valuing your worth, growing empathy, and building genuine connections.

Respectful and Insightful Discussions on Mental Health

Have you thought about how talking about mental health can really help you and others? Mental health, especially stuff like narcissism, often gets misunderstood and carries a stigma. But discussing it respectfully and with some insight can make a huge difference in understanding ourselves and others.

Why is mental health just as important as physical health? Just like our bodies need care, so do our minds. Narcissism is one part of mental health that needs attention and understanding. Realizing this helps us treat mental health with the respect it deserves. Recognizing that mental health issues are real and need attention can lead to more empathetic and informed conversations.

Do you know how empathy can change these conversations? Empathy is all about understanding and sharing the feelings of others. It helps us connect and reduces the isolation that often comes with mental health issues. When we talk about narcissism with empathy, we break down barriers and make it easier to have open and honest discussions. This approach encourages people to share their experiences and seek the help they need.

Have you gained insight into what narcissism really is? Understanding the symptoms, causes, and effects of narcissism helps us have better conversations. This knowledge isn't something you gain once; it's an ongoing process. Staying open to new information and perspectives keeps our understanding growing and our discussions meaningful. By continuously learning, we can have more nuanced and helpful conversations about narcissism and mental health.

Why is it important to talk about mental health without judgment? Judgment can create shame and silence, stopping the open dialogue we need for understanding and healing. Creating a space of acceptance and understanding encourages people to share their experiences and seek help. When we approach mental health discussions without judgment, we foster an environment where people feel safe to express their feelings and challenges.

Do you realize how unique everyone's experience with narcissism is? Each person's journey with mental health is different. By listening to and validating different stories, we enrich our understanding and make our conversations about mental health more inclusive. This inclusivity ensures that we respect and acknowledge the diverse experiences of those dealing with narcissism and other mental health issues.

How can respectful and insightful discussions empower us? These conversations can show people with narcissism that they are not alone and that help is available. They can also educate others about what living with narcissism is like, promoting empathy and understanding. Respectful discussions help dismantle the stigma around mental health and encourage more people to seek support and treatment.

Talking openly and respectfully about mental health helps us understand

and overcome narcissism. It challenges stigma, promotes empathy, and fosters a deeper understanding of mental health. Engaging in these discussions contributes to a society that values mental health as much as physical health. This is a crucial step in stopping narcissistic behavior and promoting overall well-being.

Do you find it hard to forgive yourself for past mistakes? Forgiveness, especially self-forgiveness, is vital in moving past shame or regret. It's about recognizing mistakes without letting them define you. This acceptance fosters compassion towards yourself and others, shifting away from the self-centered view that often comes with narcissism. By practicing forgiveness, you can start to heal and build healthier relationships.

Why do we feel the need to control everything? Letting go of control involves recognizing and releasing this need, which often comes from fear of vulnerability or failure. Confronting these fears helps us embrace uncertainty and develop a more relaxed approach to life. Accepting that we cannot control everything allows us to focus on what truly matters and builds resilience.

Are you ready to start these practices? The next steps involve exercises for forgiveness and letting go of control, which are essential for overcoming narcissistic tendencies. These practices offer a path toward genuine change and emotional growth. By integrating these exercises into your daily routine, you can make meaningful progress in your journey to overcome narcissism.

Focus Section: Exercises for Forgiveness and Letting Go of Control

One effective exercise for forgiveness is to write a letter to yourself. Have you tried expressing your regrets and apologies on paper? Write about the mistakes you've made and how they've affected you and others. Acknowledge your feelings and offer yourself forgiveness. This can be a powerful way to release pent-up emotions and start the healing process. Another useful practice is mindfulness meditation. Do you spend time focusing on the present moment? Mindfulness helps you become more aware of your thoughts and feelings without judgment. By regularly practicing mindfulness, you can develop a greater sense of calm and clarity, making it easier to let go of the need for control. Consider setting small, achievable goals to gradually release control. Can you identify one area of your life where you can practice letting go? Start with something manageable, like allowing others to make decisions or accepting that not everything will go as planned. Reflect on how this makes you feel and the impact it has on your stress levels and relationships.

Lastly, seek support from others. Have you talked to friends, family, or a therapist about your struggles with control and forgiveness? Sharing your journey with trusted individuals can provide valuable insights and encouragement. They can offer different perspectives and help you stay accountable to your goals.

By consistently practicing these exercises, you can begin to forgive yourself and let go of the need for control. This will help you develop a more balanced and compassionate approach to life, reducing narcissistic behaviors and improving your relationships.

Exercises for Forgiveness and Letting Go of Control

- **Daily Reflection and Journaling**: Start or end your day by reflecting on moments you felt the urge to control outcomes or struggled to forgive. Write about these instances in your journal, exploring the emotions behind these urges. This practice encourages self-awareness and understanding of your patterns.
- **Mindfulness Meditation**: Allocate time each day for mindfulness meditation, focusing on your breath and present sensations. When thoughts about past regrets or future worries arise, acknowledge them without judgment and gently return your focus to the breath. This practice helps cultivate a state of being that is anchored in the present, reducing the impulse to control.
- **Gratitude Exercises**: Every morning or evening, list three things you're grateful for. This can shift focus from what's lacking or the desire to control everything to appreciation for the present moment and what you already have.
- **Forgiveness Letters**: Write letters of forgiveness to yourself or others, even if you never send them. These letters allow you to

articulate feelings of hurt, acknowledge your role, and express a desire to forgive, fostering emotional release and healing.
- **Role-play Scenarios**: With a therapist or a trusted support person, enact scenarios where you relinquish control or practice forgiveness. These role-plays can offer insights into your emotional responses and provide a safe space to explore different ways of interacting.

Incorporating these exercises into your journey toward overcoming narcissistic behaviors offers a practical toolkit for fostering self-awareness, compassion, and a healthier way of relating to yourself and others. It's a transformative process that requires patience and commitment but promises profound growth and fulfillment as its reward.

Remember, the goal of these practices is not to change overnight but to gradually build a foundation of self-awareness, forgiveness, and openness that supports lasting change. By dedicating yourself to these exercises, you're taking significant steps toward a more balanced, empathetic, and fulfilling life.

HEALING THE INNER CHILD

Have you ever thought about how your childhood affects your behavior today? The concept of an "inner child" might seem abstract, but it represents the early part of ourselves that carries our childhood experiences, both good and bad. Comforting and healing this inner child is essential for self-awareness and personal growth.

From our earliest years, experiences shape who we are. They influence how we respond to situations, how we see ourselves, and how we view the world. When childhood experiences include neglect, criticism, or unmet emotional needs, these wounds carry into adulthood. Our inner child holds these scars, which can show up as insecurities, narcissistic behaviors, or self-sabotage.

Why is recognizing your inner child important? Acknowledging this part of ourselves is the first step to healing. This inner child is the one who delighted in play, craved love and approval, and felt pain and confusion when life was tough. Taking time each day to reflect quietly helps us connect with this youthful part of our being.

Do you ever wonder why you react a certain way? Our outbursts of anger, jealousy, or harshness can be cries for attention from our inner child. This part of us might feel neglected or unheard. Engaging with our inner child requires patience and compassion. Revisiting uncomfortable or painful memories helps us understand these feelings better.

How can you comfort your inner child? Visualization exercises are one method. Imagine offering kindness and support to your younger self. Journaling can also be a dialogue with your inner child, allowing you to express hidden hurts and longings. Engaging in activities you once loved can reconnect you with the joy and simplicity of your childhood.

Have you noticed changes in yourself as you begin this healing process? You might find that your need for external validation decreases, your empathy for others deepens, and your relationships become more genuine. This happens because you start interacting from a place of healing rather than pain or defensiveness.

Why is this process important for overcoming narcissism? Healing your inner child helps you move away from self-centered behaviors. It encourages you to be less defensive and more open to life's experiences. This journey is not a quick fix but a gradual change that requires patience and commitment. Think of it like a tree growing from a seed. The growth happens from the inside out.

What are the next steps in this journey? We will explore practical steps to begin this healing process. Every journey starts with a single step—a step of willingness to grow, change, and embrace who you can become. By comforting and healing your inner child, you lay the foundation for a self that is more balanced, empathetic, and connected with others.

Visualization exercises are powerful tools in this healing process. Have you tried imagining yourself as a child and offering comfort and understanding to that younger version of yourself? This can help bridge the gap between past wounds and present healing. Journaling is another effective method. Writing letters to your inner child, expressing love, understanding, and forgiveness, can release long-held emotions and start the healing process.

Do you remember the activities you loved as a child? Engaging in these activities again can bring joy and reconnect you with simpler, happier times. This can be anything from drawing, playing a sport, or even simple acts like playing with toys. These activities remind your inner child that it is safe and loved.

Why is patience important in this journey? Healing is not instant. It requires consistent effort and a compassionate approach. As you continue to nurture your inner child, you will notice a gradual shift in your adult self. You may become more resilient, understanding, and less reliant on external validation.

Addressing Childhood Emotional Neglect

Have you ever felt that parts of your childhood still affect how you feel and act today? Addressing childhood emotional neglect is like piecing together a mosaic of one's past. Each small piece represents a memory, a feeling, or a moment of longing for attention that went unnoticed. For many, these pieces form a picture of an inner child left in the shadows, yearning for a light that never came.

How does childhood neglect affect us as adults? The repercussions of such neglect often linger far into adulthood, manifesting as an insatiable thirst for validation or a fortress of self-protection that keeps others at a distance. It's a silent dance of seeking and retreating that can lead to a spectrum of narcissistic behaviors, where the neglected child still seeks the attention and care they were once denied. To heal, we must first acknowledge this neglect, recognizing that our unmet emotional needs from childhood could be driving forces behind our adult actions. This realization isn't an invitation to blame or wallow in what was or wasn't received from caregivers. Instead, it's an empowering moment of reclaiming agency over our emotional well-being.

What steps can you take to address this neglect? The journey to address this neglect involves cultivating a supportive and attentive relationship with oneself. It means becoming the caregiver we needed, listening to the inner child's voice, and validating its emotions. This self-parenting process can be challenging; it may require revisiting moments of vulnerability that were previously locked away. Yet, this process is also where healing begins. Creating a sacred space for reflection can aid in this healing. In the quiet corners of our days, we can sit with our younger selves, offering the compassion and understanding that was missing. Here, in the quiet, we can let our inner child speak of the loneliness, the fears, and the desires that were ignored or unfulfilled.

How can you balance reflection with action? As we listen, we not only acknowledge the past pain but also celebrate the resilience that led us here. It's important to honor the ways we navigated through those early emotional landscapes. This balanced reflection helps in recognizing not just the pain but also the strength and adaptability we've shown.

This self-reflective practice is a profound act of self-love. It's about rewriting the narrative, not as a victim of neglect but as a survivor crafting a new chapter. It's about replacing the voice that says, "I wish I had received more love," with "I am capable of giving love—to myself and to others." Like the growth of a tree, the process is not instantaneous. It requires patience, consistent care, and the willingness to embrace both the darkness and the light within. The seed of self-compassion, once planted, needs support. Over time, the once-neglected inner child begins to flourish, transforming into a self-assured adult who no longer seeks external approval but finds fulfillment within.

What does this transformation look like? This transformation isn't marked by dramatic revelations but by subtle shifts—a softening of the heart towards oneself, a gradual opening to the love of others, and a gentle release of the relentless drive for recognition. This change allows you to become more balanced and present in your relationships and daily life.

Are you ready to offer kindness to your inner child? The next steps in this journey will guide you through practical exercises and reflections to deepen this healing work, moving you closer to a self that is whole, healed, and brimming with potential. Practical exercises include visualization techniques where you imagine comforting your younger self, writing letters of compassion and understanding to your inner child, and engaging in activities that brought you joy as a child. These steps will help you reconnect with your inner child and begin the healing process.

Each step you take in comforting your inner child helps build a foundation for a healthier, more fulfilling life. This process of self-parenting, reflection, and compassion is essential for overcoming the effects of childhood emotional neglect and moving towards a more balanced and empathetic self.

Techniques for Inner Child Healing

Do you ever feel like your childhood experiences still shape your actions today? Healing the inner child, a concept that may sound like a tender return to simpler times, is actually a courageous journey into the heart of our past. It's a path lined with techniques that help soothe and repair the parts of ourselves that have been long neglected.

What does your younger self need to hear? One of the most powerful techniques for healing the inner child is visualization. Close your eyes and imagine meeting your younger self. This is a safe space where you can offer comfort, understanding, and the unconditional love your inner child may have missed. Words of affirmation that reassure them of their worth and potential can be incredibly healing. Writing to your younger self can also be very healing. Dialoguing with the inner child can be done through journaling or therapeutic conversations. By writing letters to your younger self, you create a bridge between your current self-awareness and your past innocence. Express apologies, offer support, and build a supportive relationship with the part of you that still resides in those formative years.

Do you remember what brought you joy as a child? Creative expression is another way to connect with and heal your inner child. Engage in activities that sparked joy in your younger years, whether it's drawing, dancing, or playing. These actions aren't about regressing; they're about reconnecting with a part of you that may have been silenced. They serve as reminders that joy doesn't need to be complicated or conditional. Unmet emotional needs from childhood can carry over into adulthood. For many, the inner child carries the burden of these unmet needs. Attending to these needs now—whether through self-care routines, setting healthy boundaries, or finding joy in everyday moments—can address past neglect. It's about doing for yourself what you wished others had done for you.

How would you treat yourself if you were your own parent? A particularly effective technique is the practice of self-parenting. This involves guiding yourself with the compassion and understanding you would offer a beloved child. When you feel the urge to criticize yourself, pause and consider what guidance you would offer a child. This shift in perspective can soften self-judgment and open the door to more supportive self-dialogue. Patience with yourself is vital in this healing process. Just as a seed does not become a tree overnight, your inner child will not heal in an instant. It's a gradual process, a tender support, and a compassionate journey back to the self. This ongoing effort is essential for genuine healing and growth. As we progress through this book, we will build upon these foundational techniques. Each chapter is designed to equip you with the tools you need to heal and to move forward with a renewed sense of wholeness and vitality. With each step, we affirm our commitment to support our inner child and, by extension, our entire being. This journey requires patience, compassion, and dedication, but the rewards are profound.

Taking this step to offer kindness to your inner child starts now. Practical exercises such as visualizing comforting your younger self, writing supportive letters, engaging in joyful activities, meeting your unmet emotional needs, and practicing self-parenting contribute to this healing journey. Remember, this is a gradual process, and it's important to be patient and kind to yourself as you move forward.

Re-parenting for a Positive Self-Image

Re-parenting oneself is an act of rebirth, a chance to offer the guidance, love, and support that perhaps we didn't receive at the critical stages of our development. It's a profound form of self-love that requires us to step into the roles of both parent and child, fostering a positive self-image that nurtures our growth and heals old wounds.

This journey begins by acknowledging that our self-image is often a reflection of the messages we received during our youth. Were we told we were capable and valuable, or were our efforts met with criticism and our faults highlighted? Through re-parenting, we address these imbalanced narratives, affirming our worth and rewriting the internal dialogue that can often skew toward the negative. How do we start this process? It can be as simple as changing the tone of our self-talk. Instead of criticism, we offer encouragement. Where we find fault, we also look for strength. We celebrate our successes with the same enthusiasm a proud parent would and meet our failures with compassion, not condemnation. It's essential to set aside time for this practice, to be fully present with ourselves. In these moments of solitude, we can look at our reflection—not just the physical one, but the image we hold of ourselves in our mind's eye—and begin to adjust it. We can ask ourselves what we needed but didn't receive, and then actively work to provide it. This might mean setting new boundaries, asserting our needs, or simply allowing ourselves the grace to rest. An effective re-parenting strategy involves supporting activities that bolster our self-esteem and self-worth. This could be engaging in hobbies that make us feel accomplished, pursuing new educational paths, or just allowing ourselves to play and experience joy without judgment. Engaging in activities that bring joy and satisfaction helps reinforce a positive self-image. As we re-parent, it's crucial to cultivate an environment that mirrors a nurturing home. This may mean creating spaces of comfort and safety where we can explore our emotions and desires without fear. It might involve surrounding ourselves with people who uplift us and reflecting on relationships that mirror the positive reinforcements we aim to give ourselves.

What are the boundaries that protect us? We must also learn to set internal boundaries. Just as a good parent would protect their child from harmful influences, we must protect ourselves from our own detrimental thoughts and behaviors. It's about acknowledging when we are pushing ourselves too hard or engaging in negative self-talk and consciously choosing to step back and offer kindness instead. Patience is indeed a virtue in this process. The seeds of change are sown with gentle hands and a steadfast heart. Over time, as we consistently apply these techniques of re-parenting, our self-image begins to shift. We start to see ourselves not as a collection of past failures or shortcomings, but as individuals of inherent worth and potential, deserving of love and happiness.

As we continue this journey, it's important to remember that re-parenting is not about perfection but progress. Each step forward is a victory. Whether it's waking up each day with a kind word to yourself or finding joy in simple activities, every action counts. It's about building a foundation of self-love and respect that can withstand the challenges of life.

We will explore more steps on this path to transformation as we progress through this book. Each step builds upon the last, creating a scaffold of self-love, self-respect, and the courage to face the world with a renewed sense of self. Your commitment to this transformative process is the key to unlocking your true potential. Your inner child, your past, and your future self are all awaiting your commitment to this transformative process. By re-parenting yourself, you take control of your narrative, creating a story where you are the hero who overcame adversity with love and compassion.

CHAPTER 3
YOUR INNER CHILD

Think about the times you've felt overly defensive or reacted strongly to a small issue. I know these reactions might not just be about the present situation but could be tied to a wounded inner child. The inner child is really important for emotional health and relationships. When your inner child is hurt or neglected, it can lead to behaviors aimed at protecting yourself from more pain. Unfortunately, these defensive behaviors often look a lot like narcissism. For example, if your inner child felt ignored or undervalued, you might seek constant attention or validation as an adult to fill that void. Makes sense, right?

A wounded inner child often carries unresolved emotions like fear, anger, or sadness, which can affect how you interact with others. In relationships, this can show up as a need to control situations or people to avoid feeling vulnerable. You might push others away to protect yourself from getting hurt, or you might demand too much attention and praise to feel secure. These defense mechanisms your inner child developed to cope with pain can harm your relationships and emotional health as an adult. I hear you, it's tough.

Recognizing and healing your inner child is crucial for breaking these patterns. When you understand that your defensive or narcissistic behaviors are rooted in past hurts, you can approach them with empathy and start to change. I get it, this process isn't easy, but it involves acknowledging the pain your inner child experienced and giving yourself the compassion and support you needed back then. It's about validating your own feelings and learning to express them in healthier ways. Absolutely, it takes time and effort.

By addressing the needs of your inner child, you create a foundation for healthier relationships. You become more open and less reactive, allowing for deeper connections with others. This journey of healing and understanding transforms not only how you see yourself but also how you interact with the world. You learn to replace defensive behaviors with genuine empathy and understanding, improving your emotional health and fostering stronger, more fulfilling relationships. You got this!

Why It Matters

Think about the times you've felt overly defensive or reacted strongly to a small issue. These reactions might not just be about the present situation but could be tied to a wounded inner child. I know it might sound a bit strange, but the inner child is really important for emotional health and relationships. When your inner child is hurt or neglected, it can lead to behaviors aimed at protecting yourself from more pain. Sadly, these defensive behaviors often look a lot like narcissism. For example, if your inner child felt ignored or undervalued, you might seek constant attention or validation as an adult to fill that void.

A wounded inner child often carries unresolved emotions like fear, anger, or sadness, which can affect how you interact with others. In relationships, this can show up as a need to control situations or people to avoid feeling vulnerable. You might push others away to protect yourself from getting hurt, or you might demand too much attention and praise to feel secure. These defense mechanisms that your inner child developed to cope with pain can harm your relationships and emotional health as an adult.

Recognizing and healing your inner child is crucial for breaking these patterns. When you understand that your defensive or narcissistic behaviors are rooted in past hurts, you can approach them with empathy and start to change. I get it, this process isn't easy, but it involves acknowledging the pain your inner child experienced and giving yourself the compassion and support you needed back then. It's about validating your own feelings and learning to express them in healthier ways.

By addressing the needs of your inner child, you create a foundation for healthier relationships. You become more open and less reactive, allowing for deeper connections with others. This journey of healing and understanding transforms not only how you see yourself but also how you interact with the world. You learn to replace defensive behaviors with genuine empathy and understanding, improving your emotional health and fostering stronger, more fulfilling relationships.

IDENTIFYING YOUR INNER CHILD

Imagine a part of you that still feels the joys and fears you experienced as a child. I know it might seem a bit odd, but this part, known as your inner child, holds the key to understanding many of your current behaviors and emotions. Recognizing the presence of your inner child is the first step in this healing journey, so here are some practical ways to start connecting with this often-hidden part of yourself.

First, pay attention to your reactions. Notice when you feel overly defensive, anxious, or reactive in situations that don't seem to warrant such strong emotions. Honestly, these intense feelings can be signals from your inner child. For example, if you feel extreme anger when someone criticizes you, it might be because your inner child felt criticized and unloved in the past.

To begin recognizing your inner child, try recalling childhood memories. Spend a few quiet moments thinking about your early experiences. What made you happy? What made you sad or scared? Write these memories down in a journal so you can see patterns and understand the roots of your current emotions and behaviors. Sounds good?

Another helpful exercise is to look at old photographs of yourself as a child. As you look at these pictures, try to remember how you felt at that time. What were your hopes and fears? What did you need from the adults around you? This visual connection can make it easier to empathize with your inner child and understand their ongoing influence on your life.

Engage in activities you enjoyed as a child. Did you love drawing, playing with toys, or running outside? Spend some time doing these activities again, and they can help you reconnect with your inner child and bring back positive feelings from your past. For example, if you loved building with blocks, try spending a few minutes creating something with Legos. This playful activity can open a pathway to those buried emotions and memories.

Talking to your inner child is another powerful exercise. Find a quiet space, close your eyes, and imagine your younger self sitting in front of you. What would you say to comfort and reassure them? Speak to your inner child with kindness and understanding. You might say, "I know you felt lonely sometimes, but I'm here now and you're not alone." This dialogue can help you build a supportive relationship with your inner child. I know, it feels right.

Finally, practice self-awareness throughout your day. When you feel strong emotions, pause and ask yourself, "Is this my adult self reacting, or is it my inner child?" This question can help you separate your current self from past experiences, making it easier to respond with understanding and care.

RECOGNIZING YOUR INNER CHILD

Signs of a Wounded Inner Child

Ever wonder why certain situations make you feel unexpectedly upset or anxious? I get it; these reactions might be signs of a wounded inner child, and recognizing them can help you understand and heal from past emotional wounds. One common sign is feeling overly defensive or sensitive to criticism. If someone's comment feels like a personal attack, it might be because your inner child feels vulnerable. For instance, when you get really upset if your boss gives you feedback, it could be because your inner child felt criticized or unappreciated back in the day. Makes sense, right?

Having trouble trusting others is another sign of a wounded inner child. If you find it hard to rely on people or believe they genuinely care about you, it might be your inner child's fear of being hurt again. This lack of trust often comes from past experiences where your trust was broken. I hear you, it's tough to open up, but recognizing this can be the first step toward healing.

You might also feel unworthy or not good enough, especially if you often think you're not smart enough, attractive enough, or successful enough. This might be your inner child talking because you were made to feel inadequate or if your efforts weren't acknowledged. For example, when you were always compared to others as a kid, you might still carry those feelings. Fair enough?

Struggling with intimacy and close relationships can also point to a wounded inner child, especially if getting close to people or maintaining relationships is hard. Your inner child might fear abandonment or rejection, so this fear can make you keep people at a distance to protect yourself. I get it, it's a defense mechanism developed over time.

Emotional triggers are another big clue. When certain situations or comments make you feel unusually angry, sad, or anxious, it might be your inner child reacting to old wounds. For example, if a partner's mild criticism brings up intense anger, it might be a reaction to feeling criticized and unloved in the past. That's right, it can be deep-rooted and often hard to shake off.

Feeling a strong need for control is also a sign. When you feel you must control everything around you to feel safe, it could be your inner child trying to prevent chaos and insecurity. This behavior often develops from growing up in an unpredictable or unsafe environment. No doubt about it, control can be a way to cope.

Finally, frequent feelings of guilt or shame can indicate a wounded inner child. If you often feel guilty for things that aren't your fault or ashamed of who you are, these feelings might be rooted in childhood experiences. For instance, if you were blamed for family problems as a child, you might still carry that undeserved guilt. I see what you mean, it's a heavy burden to carry.

Understanding Behavior Patterns

Ever wonder why you act a certain way in certain situations? I know it can be puzzling, but many behaviors we exhibit as adults can be traced back to wounds from our childhood. These past experiences shape our current actions, sometimes without us even realizing it.

Think about times when you've felt the need to constantly prove yourself. This behavior often stems from a childhood where you felt you had to earn love or approval. If your parents or caregivers only showed affection when you achieved something, you might have learned to tie your self-worth to accomplishments. So now, as an adult, you might push yourself to the limit, seeking validation through success because that's how you learned to feel valued.

Or consider the times when you find it hard to open up in relationships. If you experienced betrayal or neglect as a child, it's natural to build walls to protect yourself from getting hurt again. These walls might manifest as difficulty in trusting others or fear of intimacy. For instance, if a parent was emotionally unavailable, you might find it challenging to share your feelings, fearing that others will also let you down.

Have you ever noticed how some people react intensely to criticism? This can be traced back to times when they were made to feel not good enough. If, as a child, you were frequently criticized or compared to others, you might have developed a heightened sensitivity to criticism. Now, any negative feedback might feel like a personal attack, causing you to react defensively.

Another behavior that has roots in childhood is the tendency to avoid conflict. If you grew up in a household where conflicts were explosive or unresolved, you might have learned to keep the peace at all costs. As an adult, this can lead to avoiding necessary confrontations or suppressing your own needs to avoid upsetting others. For example, you might agree with others just to keep things smooth, even if you don't truly agree because that's how you maintained safety growing up.

Do you find yourself constantly seeking approval? This can be linked to a need for external validation formed in childhood. If you only received positive attention when pleasing others, you might have learned to prioritize others' needs over your own. As an adult, this might look like always saying yes, even when you want to say no because you crave that validation.

Understanding these connections is key to breaking unhealthy patterns. Recognizing that your adult behaviors often stem from childhood experiences allows you to address the root cause. Instead of just dealing with the symptoms, you can heal the original wounds. This awareness is the first step toward making conscious changes and building healthier, more fulfilling relationships.

Self-Assessment Exercises

Have you ever caught yourself reacting in ways that seem a bit over the top, and then wondered where that came from? I know, it can be puzzling. Let's dive into some self-assessment exercises to help you identify how your inner child might be influencing your current behavior. These exercises are designed to be straightforward and insightful, so let's get started.

Exercise 1: Emotional Triggers Journal

Grab a notebook or open a new document on your phone. For the next week, jot down any time you feel a strong emotional reaction. Write what happened, how you felt, and what it reminded you of from your past. Maybe your boss criticized your work, and you felt a wave of anger. Did it remind you of how you felt when your efforts weren't acknowledged as a kid? Reflect on these patterns, as this can give you insights into how your inner child is influencing your responses.

Exercise 2: Imaginary Conversation

Sit in a quiet place and close your eyes. Imagine talking to your younger self. Picture yourself at a specific age when you remember feeling hurt, scared, or unappreciated. What would you say to comfort that child now? For example, if you remember feeling left out at a young age, tell your younger self that it's okay to feel that way and that they are important. This exercise can help bridge the gap between past and present emotions.

Exercise 3: Mirror Exercise

Stand in front of a mirror and look at yourself. Speak to your reflection as if you're talking to your younger self. You might say something like, "Hey, I know you went through a lot back then, and it's okay to feel those emotions. You're strong, and you've grown so much." This practice helps you connect with your inner child and validate their feelings.

Exercise 4: Visualization

Find a comfortable spot, close your eyes, and take a few deep breaths. Visualize a safe place where your inner child feels secure and loved. It could be a cozy room, a sunny beach, or anywhere that feels peaceful. Imagine your younger self there, happy and carefree. Spend a few minutes in this visualization, reminding yourself that your inner child deserves love and safety. This exercise can help you feel more grounded and compassionate toward yourself.

Exercise 5: Trigger Identification

Think about recent conflicts or situations that triggered a strong emotional response. Write down what happened and how you felt. Next, reflect on any past experiences that might have caused similar feelings. For instance, if you felt abandoned when your partner didn't respond to your texts, does it remind you of times when you felt neglected as a child? Connecting these dots can help you understand your reactions better.

Exercise 6: Self-Compassion Letter

Write a letter to yourself from the perspective of a kind and understanding friend. Acknowledge any struggles or pain your inner child has experienced and offer words of comfort and encouragement. You might write, "I know you've been through tough times, and it's okay to feel hurt. You're doing your best, and that's enough." This letter can be a powerful tool for nurturing your inner child and fostering self-compassion.

These exercises are simple but can provide profound insights into how your inner child influences your current behavior. By reflecting on your emotions, visualizing safety, and practicing self-compassion, you can begin to heal old wounds and build a healthier relationship with yourself. Remember, it's a journey, and every step you take is a move toward understanding and growth. Keep going; you've got this.

THE IMPACT OF A WOUNDED INNER CHILD ON NARCISSISTIC BEHAVIOR

Emotional Well-Being and Relationships

Ever notice how some emotional reactions seem a bit extreme for the situation? I know, it can be confusing. When your inner child is wounded, it can seriously mess with your emotional well-being and relationships. Let's break it down.

First, your emotional state is directly affected. A wounded inner child often leads to feelings of insecurity, low self-esteem, and unresolved anger, which can bubble up and affect your day-to-day life, making you feel overwhelmed or anxious without clear reasons. For instance, you might find yourself getting unusually upset over minor criticisms or feeling constantly on edge because of these underlying emotional issues.

These emotional problems spill over into your relationships as well. When your inner child is hurt, you might struggle with trust and intimacy, making it hard to open up to others and fearing rejection or betrayal. Consequently, this can create a barrier between you and your loved ones, making genuine connections difficult. For example, you might push people away or become overly clingy, trying to protect yourself from potential hurt.

Moreover, a wounded inner child can lead to defensive behaviors. When someone tries to give you constructive feedback, you might react with anger or dismissiveness, interpreting their words as personal attacks. This defensiveness can prevent healthy communication and problem-solving in your relationships. Instead of addressing issues calmly, you might escalate conflicts or withdraw, which only makes things worse.

Another significant impact is the development of narcissistic tendencies. When your inner child feels neglected or unloved, you might overcompensate by seeking constant validation and admiration from others. This need for approval can turn into narcissistic behaviors, where you prioritize your own needs and feelings over those of others. You might find yourself constantly seeking attention or reacting negatively when you don't get the recognition you crave.

Furthermore, your ability to empathize with others might be compromised. A wounded inner child can make it challenging to understand and share the feelings of others, leading to misunderstandings and conflicts. For instance, if you're always focused on protecting yourself, you might not notice when your partner is feeling neglected or upset. This lack of empathy can create a disconnect, making it hard to build and maintain strong, healthy relationships.

Lastly, these behaviors create a vicious cycle. Your relationships suffer, which in turn reinforces your inner child's wounds, making you feel even more insecure and defensive. It's a tough loop to break out of, but recognizing the patterns is the first step. By understanding how a wounded inner child affects your emotional well-being and relationships, you can start to address these issues and work towards healing.

Connection to Narcissistic Behaviors

Ever wondered why some adults act out in ways that seem, well, a bit self-centered or overly defensive? I know, it can be puzzling. This often ties back to unresolved childhood issues that manifest as narcissistic traits in adulthood. Let's dive into how this happens.

First, think about unresolved issues from childhood, like not getting enough attention or feeling unloved. These experiences can leave deep emotional scars. As adults, to protect themselves, individuals might develop narcissistic traits. For example, if a child never felt good enough or constantly sought approval, they might grow up to crave admiration and validation from others. This craving can turn into an exaggerated sense of self-importance because they're trying to fill that unmet need from childhood.

Next, let's look at control. Kids who grew up in chaotic or unpredictable environments might develop a need to control everything around them as adults. This need for control can come off as bossy or domineering. For instance, if you always had to look out for yourself because the adults around you were unreliable, you might end up trying to control every situation to feel safe. Unfortunately, this behavior can make you seem like a control freak, alienating those around you.

Moreover, consider the inability to empathize. Children who were taught to suppress their emotions or were never shown empathy might struggle to connect with others' feelings as adults. They might appear cold or indifferent because they don't know how to respond to others emotionally. For example, if you never saw your parents showing empathy, you might not have learned how to be empathetic yourself. This lack of empathy can lead to superficial relationships where deep emotional connections are missing.

Additionally, the need for constant validation can stem from childhood neglect. If you were ignored or felt invisible as a child, you might seek out attention in unhealthy ways as an adult. This might look like constantly fishing for compliments or bragging about your achievements. You're essentially trying to get the validation you never received as a kid. For instance, a person who was neglected might post excessively on social media, seeking likes and comments to feel valued.

Furthermore, defensive behaviors are another common trait. If you were often criticized or made to feel worthless as a child, you might become overly sensitive to criticism as an adult. This sensitivity can make you lash out or shut down when someone points out a flaw. For example, if a boss gives you constructive feedback and you react with anger or denial, it could be your wounded inner child feeling attacked.

Breaking the Cycle

Breaking the cycle of narcissistic behaviors begins with addressing and healing the inner child. I know it sounds like a tall order, but with the right strategies, you can make significant progress. Here's how you can get started.

First, start by acknowledging and accepting your inner child. This might feel a bit strange at first, but it's important to recognize that the hurt and pain from your childhood still affects you today. You might even talk to your inner child, reassuring them that it's okay to feel what they feel. For example, saying, "I know you felt abandoned and unloved, but I'm here now, and we're going to work through this together," can be powerful.

Next, work on identifying and understanding your triggers. These are situations or comments that make you react strongly, often in ways that seem out of proportion. When you understand what triggers these reactions, you can start to change how you respond. Keep a journal and note when you feel these intense emotions, what happened to trigger them, and how you reacted. Over time, you'll notice patterns that can help you understand the underlying issues.

Developing self-compassion is another crucial step. This means treating yourself with the same kindness and understanding that you would offer to a friend. When you make a mistake or feel overwhelmed, instead of criticizing yourself, try saying something supportive. For instance, "It's okay to feel this way. I'm learning and growing, and that's what matters." By being kind to yourself, you can start to heal the wounds of your inner child.

Moreover, practice mindfulness to stay connected to the present moment. This helps you become more aware of your thoughts and feelings without judgment. Techniques like deep breathing, meditation, or simply taking a few moments to focus on your surroundings can help you stay grounded. When you feel a strong emotion, take a few deep breaths and ask yourself what's really going on. This can help you respond more calmly and thoughtfully.

In addition, set healthy boundaries in your relationships. Learning to say no and protect your emotional well-being is essential. If someone's behavior is triggering your inner child, it's okay to step back and take care of yourself. For example, if a friend's criticism is hurting you, it's okay to say, "I need some space right now. Let's talk about this later." Boundaries help you protect yourself while you're healing.

Engage in activities that nurture and heal your inner child. This might include creative activities like drawing or painting, physical activities like playing a sport, or simply doing things you loved as a child. These activities can help you reconnect with the joyful and carefree parts of yourself. For instance, if you loved playing with Legos as a kid, spend some time building something fun. It's a great way to reconnect with that playful energy.

Furthermore, seek support from trusted friends or support groups. Talking about your experiences and feelings with others who understand can be incredibly validating and healing. They can offer support, advice, and encouragement as you work through your issues. For example, joining a support group for people recovering from narcissistic tendencies can provide a safe space to share and learn from others' experiences.

Finally, consider writing letters to your inner child. This might sound a bit odd, but it can be a powerful way to express your feelings and start healing. Write a letter to your younger self, acknowledging their pain and offering the support and understanding they needed but didn't get. For example, "Dear little me, I know you felt scared and alone, but you were so brave. I'm here now, and we're going to be okay."

Breaking the cycle of narcissistic behaviors by healing your inner child takes time and patience. But by using these strategies, you can start to make real progress. Remember, it's about taking small steps and being kind to yourself along the way. You've got this, and you're not alone on this journey.

HEALING YOUR INNER CHILD

Techniques for Emotional Healing

Healing your inner child might sound like a big task, but with the right techniques, you can make significant progress. Let's dive into some practical methods for emotional healing that are straightforward and easy to follow.

First, try journaling. I know, writing in a diary might seem old-school, but it's super effective. Grab a notebook and jot down your thoughts and feelings each day. This helps you process emotions and identify patterns. For instance, if you notice that certain situations always trigger the same feelings, you can start to understand why and work on them. Writing things down gives you a clear picture of your emotional landscape.

Another great technique is visualization. Close your eyes and picture your younger self in a safe, happy place. Imagine giving your inner child a hug and telling them they are loved and safe. This might sound a bit cheesy, but it can be incredibly comforting. Visualization helps you connect with your inner child on a deeper level, promoting healing and self-acceptance.

Engaging in creative activities is also powerful. Remember how fun it was to draw, paint, or build things as a kid? Get back into those hobbies. Creativity allows you to express emotions that words can't always capture. Plus, it's just plain fun and can bring joy back into your life. Maybe try painting a picture or building something with Legos. These activities can be surprisingly therapeutic.

Mindfulness and meditation are key, too. Take a few minutes each day to sit quietly and focus on your breath. If your mind starts to wander, gently bring it back to your breathing. This practice helps you stay present and reduces stress. It's all about giving your mind a break and just being in the moment. You might think, "I don't have time for this," but even five minutes can make a big difference.

Talk to yourself kindly. When you make a mistake or feel down, instead of beating yourself up, say something supportive. Imagine what you'd say to a friend in the same situation. For example, if you mess up at work, instead of thinking, "I'm such an idiot," try, "I had a tough day, but I'm doing my best." This shift in self-talk can significantly improve your emotional health.

Physical activity is also a great healer. Go for a walk, run, or do some yoga. Exercise releases endorphins, which are natural mood boosters. Plus, it gets you out of your head and into your body. You don't have to run a marathon – even a short walk around the block can help clear your mind and lift your spirits.

Finally, seek support from friends or join a support group. Talking about your feelings with others who understand can be incredibly validating. They can offer new perspectives and advice. Plus, knowing you're not alone in your struggles is comforting. Maybe join a group for people working on similar issues or find a friend who's a good listener.

Nurturing Your Inner Child

Nurturing your inner child is all about reconnecting with that part of yourself and giving it the care and attention it needs. I know it might sound a bit strange at first, but these practices can really make a difference in how you feel and relate to others. Here are some specific practices and exercises to help you nurture and care for your inner child.

Start with self-compassion. Treat yourself with the same kindness you would offer a friend. When you're feeling down, say something supportive to yourself. For example, if you make a mistake, instead of beating yourself up, remind yourself, "Everyone makes mistakes, and it's okay. I'm learning and growing." This kind of self-talk can really boost your self-esteem and make you feel more secure.

Next, engage in playful activities. Remember what you loved doing as a kid? Whether it was drawing, playing sports, or building things with Legos, try to incorporate some of those activities into your life now. Play is not just for kids; it's a great way to relieve stress and reconnect with your inner child. So, go ahead and pick up that coloring book or take a swing at the park. It's all about having fun and letting go.

Spend time in nature. Just like children, we often feel more relaxed and happy when we're outside. Take a walk in the park, go for a hike, or simply sit in your backyard and enjoy the fresh air. Nature has a calming effect and can help you feel more grounded. Plus, it's a great way to clear your mind and reflect on your feelings.

Practice mindfulness. Take a few minutes each day to sit quietly and focus on your breath. When your mind starts to wander, gently bring it back to your breathing. This practice helps you stay present and reduces stress. It's like giving your mind a little vacation. You might think, "I don't have time for this," but even five minutes can make a big difference.

Talk to your inner child. I know it might feel silly, but try speaking to your inner child as if they were right there with you. You can say things like, "I love you," "You are safe," or "I'm here for you." This practice helps build a stronger connection with your inner self and reinforces positive feelings. It's about creating a safe space within yourself where your inner child feels valued and loved.

Write letters to your inner child. This exercise allows you to express your feelings and thoughts in a structured way. Write about your experiences, fears, and hopes. Then, write a response from your inner child's perspective. This dialogue can help you understand your inner child's needs and how to meet them. It's a powerful way to foster self-compassion and empathy.

Surround yourself with positive influences. Spend time with people who uplift and support you. Healthy relationships can reinforce your self-worth and provide a sense of belonging. If someone constantly criticizes or undermines you, it might be best to limit your time with them. Instead, seek out friends and family who make you feel good about yourself.

Set boundaries. It's important to protect your inner child from harm. This means setting boundaries with others and yourself. If something doesn't feel right, it's okay to say no. By setting boundaries, you're telling your inner child that their well-being is important. It's about creating a safe environment where you can thrive.

Lastly, practice gratitude. Each day, write down a few things you're grateful for. This habit shifts your focus from negative thoughts to positive ones, enhancing your overall sense of well-being. Gratitude helps you appreciate the good things in your life and reduces the impact of negative thoughts.

Building Self-Love and Acceptance

Building self-love and acceptance is essential for healing your inner child and fostering overall well-being. I know it might sound easier said than done, but it's definitely possible with some practical steps and a bit of patience. Here are some tips and exercises to help you develop self-love and acceptance:

Start with positive affirmations. Stand in front of the mirror each morning and tell yourself something positive. It might feel awkward at first, but it can boost your self-esteem over time. For example, say, "I am worthy of love and respect," or "I accept myself as I am." These affirmations help counteract negative self-talk and build a positive self-image.

Practice self-care regularly. Take time out for activities that make you feel good and relaxed. Whether it's taking a long bath, reading a book, or going for a walk, self-care is all about treating yourself with kindness. You deserve to feel good, so make sure to carve out time for these activities. Remember, it's not selfish to prioritize your own needs.

Set realistic goals and celebrate your achievements. Break down your goals into smaller, manageable steps and celebrate each milestone, no matter how small. For example, if your goal is to exercise more, start with a ten-minute walk each day and gradually increase the time. Celebrating your progress, even if it's just a pat on the back, reinforces your sense of accomplishment and boosts your confidence.

Forgive yourself for past mistakes. Holding onto guilt and regret can hinder self-love. Acknowledge your mistakes, learn from them, and then let them go. Nobody's perfect, and it's okay to make mistakes. Forgiveness is a crucial step toward self-acceptance. Think of it this way: if a friend made a mistake, you'd likely forgive them. So why not extend the same kindness to yourself?

Surround yourself with positive influences. Spend time with people who uplift and support you. Healthy relationships play a significant role in developing self-love. If someone constantly brings you down, it might be best to limit your time with them. Instead, seek out friends and family who make you feel valued and appreciated.

Engage in activities that bring you joy. Doing things you love can significantly enhance your sense of self-worth. Whether it's a hobby, sports, or creative pursuits, make sure to include these activities in your routine. For example, if you love painting, set aside time each week to create art. This not only boosts your mood but also reinforces your unique talents and interests.

Reflect on your strengths and achievements. Take some time to write down your strengths, achievements, and qualities you admire in yourself. Reflecting on these positive aspects can help you appreciate who you are. Whenever you feel down, revisit this list to remind yourself of your worth and capabilities.

Practice gratitude daily. Each day, write down three things you are grateful for. This habit shifts your focus from negative thoughts to positive ones, enhancing your overall sense of well-being. Gratitude helps you appreciate the good things in your life and reduces the impact of negative self-talk.

Seek inspiration from others. Read books or listen to podcasts about self-love and personal growth. Learning from others' experiences can provide valuable insights and motivation. For example, you might find comfort and guidance in reading about how others overcame their struggles with self-acceptance.

Finally, be patient with yourself. Developing self-love and acceptance is a journey, and it's okay to have setbacks. Treat yourself with the same compassion you would offer a friend going through a tough time. Remind yourself that growth takes time, and every step forward, no matter how small, is progress.

CREATIVE EXPRESSION AND PLAY

Role of Creative Activities

Ever noticed how doodling or playing around with creative projects can instantly lift your mood? Engaging in creative activities isn't just fun; it's a powerful way to heal and express your inner feelings. When you dive into activities like painting, drawing, writing, or even building something, you're not just creating art – you're also tapping into a deeper part of yourself that needs expression.

Creative activities play a crucial role in the healing process because they provide an outlet for emotions that might be hard to express otherwise. Think about it: when you're feeling stressed or upset, putting your thoughts and feelings into a creative project can be incredibly freeing. It's like having a conversation with yourself, but through colors, shapes, and words instead of just thoughts.

For example, painting can be a fantastic way to express emotions. The act of choosing colors, applying brushstrokes, and seeing your feelings come to life on canvas can be incredibly therapeutic. If you've had a rough day, grabbing some paints and a canvas can help you unwind and process what's going on inside.

Similarly, writing can also be a powerful tool for healing. Keeping a journal where you jot down your thoughts, experiences, and dreams can help you make sense of your emotions. It doesn't have to be perfect – just let the words flow. You might be surprised at how much clarity you gain by simply writing things down.

Engaging in play is equally important. Remember how much fun you had as a kid playing with toys or inventing games? Bringing a sense of play into your life as an adult can help you reconnect with your inner child. Whether it's playing a musical instrument, building with LEGO bricks, or just goofing around with friends, play helps you relax and enjoy the moment.

Creative expression and play are not just hobbies; they're essential for emotional well-being. They offer a break from the daily grind and a chance to connect with your true self. Moreover, they can help you build resilience by providing a healthy way to cope with stress and challenges.

So, next time you feel overwhelmed, try picking up a paintbrush, writing a story, or simply playing a game. These activities can help you process your emotions, boost your mood, and ultimately, heal your inner child. And remember, it's not about creating a masterpiece – it's about expressing yourself and having fun. Give it a try and see how it transforms your day!

Incorporating Play into Daily Life

Ever feel like life's all work and no play? I know, it's easy to get caught up in responsibilities and forget the joy that play can bring. Incorporating play into your daily routine isn't just for kids – it's essential for your emotional health and healing. Play can help you relax, reduce stress, and bring a sense of fun and adventure back into your life.

Think about the last time you laughed so hard your stomach hurt. That kind of joy is incredibly therapeutic. Playing can be as simple as taking a break to toss a ball around, playing a board game, or engaging in a hobby you love. For example, if you enjoy music, take a few minutes each day to play an instrument or listen to your favorite songs. This can lift your spirits and provide a much-needed break from the daily grind.

You don't need a lot of time or fancy equipment to incorporate play into your day. Start with small, fun activities that fit into your routine. For instance, take a short walk and pay attention to the sights and sounds around you, or play a quick game of catch with a friend or family member. Even something as simple as doodling or coloring can be a form of play that helps you relax and express yourself creatively.

Moreover, playing can help strengthen relationships. Sharing a game or playful activity with someone can build bonds and improve communication. For example, playing a game of cards or a board game with your family can create a fun and relaxed atmosphere where everyone feels connected and engaged. It's a great way to unwind and enjoy each other's company.

Including play in your day also boosts creativity and problem-solving skills.

When you allow yourself to play, you give your brain a chance to think in new ways and come up with creative solutions. This can be particularly helpful if you're feeling stuck or overwhelmed by challenges. For instance, taking a break to engage in a playful activity can refresh your mind and help you return to tasks with a new perspective.

To make play a regular part of your life, schedule it into your day just like any other important activity. Set aside a specific time each day to do something fun, whether it's playing a sport, engaging in a hobby, or just goofing around. This consistent practice can greatly enhance your emotional well-being and provide a sense of balance.

Practical Exercises for Creative Expression

Feeling a bit stuck creatively? I know, it happens to the best of us. Here are some practical exercises to help you tap into your creative side and add a bit of play to your day. These activities can boost your emotional well-being and bring a smile to your face. Let's dive in!

Doodle Time Grab a piece of paper and a pen, and just start doodling. Don't worry about what it looks like; the point is to let your mind wander and express itself freely. Set a timer for 10 minutes and see what you come up with. You might surprise yourself with a fun design or an interesting pattern.

Story Cubes If you've never tried story cubes, you're in for a treat. Roll a set of story dice and use the pictures that come up to create a short story. This can be a fun solo activity or something you do with friends or family. It's a great way to spark your imagination and see where your creativity takes you.

Music Jam Session Whether you play an instrument or just love to sing along to your favorite tunes, a jam session can be incredibly therapeutic. Put on some music and let yourself get lost in the rhythm. Don't worry about how you sound; the goal is to have fun and express yourself.

Nature Walk with a Twist Take a walk outside and make it a game. Look for objects that match each color of the rainbow or try to spot things that start with each letter of the alphabet. This adds a playful element to your walk and helps you see the world in a new way.

Collage Creation Gather old magazines, newspapers, or printouts and create a collage. Cut out pictures, words, and phrases that catch your eye and glue them onto a piece of paper to make a new piece of art. This can be a relaxing way to express your thoughts and feelings visually.

Character Swap Write a short story or scene where you swap roles with someone you know or a character from a book or movie. Imagine how they would handle a situation you're dealing with. This exercise can be both fun and enlightening, giving you new perspectives on your own life.

Improv Games Try some improv games to get your creative juices flowing. One simple game is "Yes, and…" where you and a friend build a story together. One person starts with a sentence, and the next person adds on, always starting with "Yes, and…" This keeps the story going and encourages creative thinking.

DIY Craft Projects Pick a simple craft project like making a friendship bracelet, painting a rock, or building a birdhouse. Follow the instructions or let your creativity guide you. These projects can be a great way to relax and create something beautiful.

Gratitude Art Journal Combine art and gratitude by keeping a journal where you draw or collage something you're grateful for each day. This practice not only boosts your creativity but also helps you focus on the positive aspects of your life.

Mindful Coloring Coloring isn't just for kids; it's a great way to unwind and tap into your creative side. Get an adult coloring book or print out some intricate designs online. Spend a few minutes coloring each day to relax and let your mind wander.

Give these exercises a try and see which ones resonate with you. Incorporating creative expression and play into your daily routine can bring joy, reduce stress, and help you connect with your inner child. So, go ahead and have some fun with it!

CHAPTER 4
ADDRESSING CORE NARCISSISTIC BEHAVIORS

Small steps lead to big changes.

BREAKING THE NARCISSISTIC CYCLE

Do you ever notice certain behaviors in yourself that hurt your relationships? To improve, we need to spot these habits, much like finding weeds in a garden before they take over. These habits, formed over many years, can damage our connections with others and stop our personal growth. Breaking the narcissistic cycle starts with noticing these patterns and being willing to change them.

Do you sometimes dismiss criticism quickly, blame others, always seek praise, or struggle to empathize? These behaviors might have protected you at some point, but now they block deeper connections with others and yourself.

How can we start breaking these habits? First, we need to be very aware of ourselves. This means creating time to think about our actions and reactions. Ask yourself questions like, "Was my response fair?" or "Am I listening to understand or just to reply?" This isn't about blaming yourself but about honestly looking at your behavior.

One helpful way to spot these patterns is by keeping a journal. Writing down moments when you notice narcissistic behaviors can help you see patterns that aren't clear in the moment. Over time, this journal can show your progress and highlight what triggers these behaviors. Talking with trusted friends or a therapist can also help. They can offer perspectives that you might not see. These conversations might be uncomfortable, but they are very helpful for change. When you identify these behaviors, challenge them. If you feel like dominating a conversation, try to pause and let others speak. If criticism makes you defensive, take a breath and respond with curiosity instead of anger. These moments of choice are where real change starts. Remember, breaking long-standing habits takes time. It requires patience, persistence, and self-kindness. Mistakes and setbacks are part of the journey. They are not failures but chances to learn and grow.

As we move forward, we will look at strategies for mindfulness and behavior changes that support this process. Every step in breaking the narcissistic cycle opens up new paths for personal growth and healthier relationships.

Are you ready to face the challenge and start this transformative path?

Behavior Modification Strategies

How can we change deeply ingrained narcissistic behaviors? It takes more than just understanding; it requires action. Behavior modification strategies provide practical steps to help us make these changes. These strategies help us change how we react, interact, and see ourselves.

Do you ever find yourself reacting quickly without thinking? One helpful strategy is using delay tactics. When you feel the need for immediate validation or want to judge quickly, try to pause. Even a few breaths can create a moment to think, allowing for a calmer and kinder response. Have you tried taking a moment before reacting? Setting small goals is another key strategy. Changing behavior is like a journey; it happens one step at a time. Identify specific behaviors you want to change and set small, achievable goals. Celebrate each success, no matter how small, to encourage positive change. Do you set small goals to track your progress? Do you find it helpful to write things down? Keeping a journal can help you spot patterns in your behavior. Write down when you notice narcissistic behaviors, what triggered them, how you reacted, and how you felt. This self-reflection can show patterns and help you understand why certain behaviors continue. It also lets you see your progress over time. Have you tried journaling to track your behavior? Positive reinforcement is important too. Reward yourself when you handle a situation in a non-narcissistic way. Understanding the negative consequences of narcissistic behaviors, like strained relationships, can also motivate you to change. How do you reward your positive behaviors?

Getting feedback from trusted friends or a therapist can further enhance your efforts. They can provide valuable insights and constructive criticism. This external perspective can help you see your behavior more clearly and encourage deeper change. Do you seek feedback to improve your behavior? Remember, setbacks are part of the process. They are not failures but chances to learn and grow. With patience, persistence, and the right strategies, change is not just possible; it's within reach.

Let's continue this journey together, exploring more tools and techniques that will support your transformation.

Celebrating Progress and Navigating Setbacks

How can we reshape our behaviors and celebrate progress while handling setbacks? Changing narcissistic behaviors is both rewarding and challenging. It needs self-awareness, patience, and resilience. Celebrating progress and seeing setbacks as part of learning are key to staying motivated and committed to change.

Celebrating Progress

Every step forward, every moment of self-awareness, and every time we choose empathy over ego is a victory worth celebrating. Do you recognize these moments in your journey? These achievements show that change is possible and help reinforce our commitment to personal growth. Celebrating progress is not about boosting our ego but about appreciating the effort and courage it takes to change.

How do you celebrate your progress? It can be as simple as reflecting on how far you've come, sharing your achievements with a friend or therapist, or treating yourself to something nice. These small acts of recognition keep us motivated and remind us why we started this journey.

1. **Managing Setbacks**: Setbacks are a normal part of any change process. They don't mean you've failed; they show that change is complex and takes time. When you face a setback, approach it with kindness and without judgment. Have you ever thought about what triggers your setbacks? Use these moments to reflect and learn.Instead of criticizing yourself, ask, "What can I learn from this?" This way, setbacks become valuable lessons. Reaffirm your commitment to change, revisit your goals, and seek support from trusted friends or therapists. They can provide encouragement and guidance.
2. **Integrating Lessons Learned**: Each setback is a chance to refine your strategies and understand your triggers better. Do you use setbacks to learn and grow? Revisiting your goals to make sure they are realistic and achievable can strengthen your resolve and keep you aligned with your values.
3. **The Path Forward**: As we move forward, let's embrace the ups and downs of this journey. Celebrate your successes, learn from your setbacks, and keep going with grace and determination. Changing narcissistic behaviors isn't a straight path. It's full of twists and turns, each offering deeper insights and the chance to become a better version of yourself.

The journey continues, and with each step, we move closer to a life of authenticity, empathy, and genuine connection. Let's proceed with courage, compassion, and the belief that we can change.

MANAGING ANGER AND CONTROL

Understanding the Roots of Narcissistic Anger

Have you ever felt like your anger just comes out of nowhere? Narcissistic anger often starts with feeling threatened. This anger usually comes from a fragile self-esteem, which might have been hurt or ignored when you were young. Do you get angry when you feel vulnerable or imperfect? This anger can stem from a fear that others will see your flaws and think less of you.

Shame is another powerful trigger for narcissistic anger. When you feel ashamed, do you react with quick and intense anger? This isn't just about defending yourself; it's about pushing away the painful feeling of not being good enough.

Control is also a big part of this anger. Do you feel like you need to control everything around you to feel safe? For someone with narcissistic traits, control feels like a lifeline. It helps them feel secure in a world that seems ready to show their vulnerabilities. When this control is challenged, the reaction can be intense anger, trying to regain dominance and feel secure again.

To manage this anger, you need to look inward and reflect on your feelings. Can you see vulnerability not as a threat but as a chance for real connection and growth? This mindset change is crucial. Therapy can help, especially those focusing on emotional intelligence and resilience. Mindfulness and self-compassion techniques can also soothe feelings of shame and inadequacy, reducing the need to lash out in anger.

Rebuilding self-esteem from the inside is another important step. Can you find worth within yourself without needing others' approval or control over them? It means accepting that imperfection is part of being human and adds to our unique value. Each setback is an opportunity to refine your strategies and understand your triggers better. Revisiting your goals to make sure they are realistic and achievable can strengthen your resolve and keep you aligned with your values. Remember, setbacks are part of the process. They don't mean you've failed; they show that change is complex and takes time. When you face a setback, approach it with kindness and without judgment. Have you ever thought about what triggers your setbacks? Use these moments to reflect and learn. Instead of criticizing yourself, ask, "What can I learn from this?" This way, setbacks become valuable lessons. Reaffirm your commitment to change, revisit your goals, and seek support from trusted friends or therapists. They can provide encouragement and guidance.

Understanding your anger, its roots, and how to manage it is the key to transforming it into a positive force for change.

Techniques for Constructive Anger Management

Managing anger constructively is key to breaking the cycle of narcissistic behavior and building healthier relationships. Anger is a natural emotion that signals when something is wrong. But how we respond to anger can either help us grow or cause harm. Let's explore techniques to turn anger from a source of conflict into a chance for positive change.

- **Acknowledgment and Acceptance**: Do you sometimes ignore your anger or react without thinking? The first step is to recognize your anger without judging yourself. Accepting your anger means understanding it as a signal, not a command to act.
- **Identify the Underlying Cause**: Have you noticed that anger often hides deeper feelings like fear, hurt, or frustration? By finding the real cause of your anger, you can deal with the true issue. This might take some honest reflection, which you can do by journaling or talking with a therapist.
- **Take a Pause**: When you feel anger rising, can you give yourself a moment to pause before reacting? Try taking deep breaths, counting to ten, or stepping away from the situation. This pause helps you respond more calmly and thoughtfully.
- **Express Anger Constructively**: Once you understand your anger, how can you express it respectfully? Use "I" statements to share your feelings without blaming others. For example, say, "I feel upset when I'm interrupted because it makes me feel unheard."
- **Seek Solutions**: Instead of focusing on what made you angry, can you work on finding a solution? Talk with the people involved to

find a compromise or a way to meet everyone's needs. This approach solves the immediate problem and prevents future issues.
- **Practice Relaxation Techniques**: Do you practice ways to stay calm? Techniques like deep breathing, meditation, or yoga can lower your overall anger and stress levels, making it easier to manage anger when it comes up.
- **Reflect and Learn**: After an anger-inducing event, do you take time to reflect on your reaction? Think about what worked well and what could be better next time. This reflection helps you learn and grow without being too hard on yourself.
- **Seek Support**: Managing anger can be tough, especially if it's a habit. Do you ask for help from friends, family, or professionals? They can offer valuable support and guidance.

These techniques help you manage anger constructively, turning it into a tool for growth and healthier relationships. As we continue, we'll explore more about facing and managing emotions positively.

RELEASING THE NEED FOR CONTROL

Why do we feel the need to control everything around us? Often, it comes from deep fears and insecurities. We think controlling outcomes and people will keep us safe, but this only distances us from real connections and inner peace. Understanding that control is a response to anxiety is crucial. Do you ever feel anxious about life's unpredictability and try to manage it by controlling things? This strategy backfires because the more we grasp for control, the more peace slips away. Embracing vulnerability and uncertainty as natural parts of life is key to releasing this need.

- **Cultivating Trust and Surrender**: Trusting yourself and others is at the heart of letting go of control. Do you believe in your ability to handle whatever comes your way? Trusting yourself means believing in your resilience. Surrendering control doesn't mean giving up; it means actively choosing to trust in the flow of life and your ability to navigate it.
- **Practicing Mindfulness**: Living in the present and accepting each moment as it is without trying to force it into what we think it should be is what mindfulness teaches us. Do you practice staying present and accepting things as they come? Mindfulness shows us that we can endure pain, disappointment, and uncertainty without needing to control everything. This awareness brings a sense of freedom and calm.
- **Embracing Uncertainty**: Do you see uncertainty as an enemy or as a source of freedom and possibility? Learning to embrace uncertainty can be transformative. It opens us up to new experiences and growth that rigid control never could. Recognizing that uncertainty can lead to positive outcomes helps diminish the fear driving our need for control.
- **Setting Healthy Boundaries**: Ironically, letting go of control involves setting and respecting healthy boundaries. Do you know where your power lies and where it doesn't? We can control our actions, reactions, and decisions, but we cannot—and should not—control others. This understanding is crucial for healthy relationships and personal well-being.
- **Seeking Support**: Letting go of control can be challenging, especially if it has been a defense mechanism for a long time. Do you seek support from therapists, support groups, or trusted friends? They can provide the guidance and reassurance needed during this process.
- **Reflecting and Re-evaluating**: Regular reflection on our behaviors and their outcomes can show us the futility of excessive control. Do you take time to reflect on your actions and their

results? This practice, combined with a willingness to learn from experiences, helps shift our perspective from one of control to one of acceptance and adaptability.

Letting go of the need for control is about embracing a new way of living that values trust, acceptance, and resilience. This journey promises profound transformation, bringing us closer to our true selves with every step.

APPROACHES TO CONFLICT RESOLUTION

Conflict is a part of human relationships. How we handle conflicts can lead to growth and understanding or to hurt and division. Dealing with conflict constructively requires a change in perspective, focusing on empathy, understanding, and mutual respect rather than winning or dominating.

- **Active Listening**: Do you fully concentrate on what others are saying, or do you just hear their words? Active listening means paying attention to words, non-verbal signals, and emotions. This helps validate the speaker's feelings and opens the way for honest communication.
- **Use "I" Statements**: Do you start sentences with "You," which can make others defensive? Try framing your concerns from your perspective. For example, say, "I feel upset when my contributions are overlooked," instead of "You always ignore my contributions." This way, you express your feelings without blaming others.
- **Seek to Understand Before Being Understood**: Do you try to understand others before explaining your own point? This principle encourages empathy and allows everyone to express their views and feelings without fear of judgment or rebuttal.

- **Focus on the Issue, Not the Person**: Do you make personal attacks during conflicts? Focus on the behavior or issue causing the conflict rather than criticizing the person. This helps create an environment where solutions are sought for the problem, not the person.
- **Agree to Disagree**: Can you accept that not all conflicts will have clear resolutions? Sometimes, agreeing to disagree respectfully can be a resolution itself. It acknowledges each person's right to their views while maintaining respect.
- **Take a Break if Needed**: Do emotions sometimes run too high during conflicts? Taking a break can prevent saying or doing something regrettable. A brief period apart can allow for cooling down and reflecting on the best way forward.
- **Collaborate on a Solution**: Do you approach conflict with the mindset of finding a "win-win" solution? This means both parties feel heard, validated, and part of the resolution. Collaborative problem-solving fosters teamwork and mutual respect.
- **Apologize When Appropriate**: Do you apologize sincerely when necessary? A genuine apology can heal the rifts caused by conflict. It shows recognition of your role in the dispute and a desire to make amends and move forward.

Managing conflict with mindfulness, empathy, and a genuine desire for resolution offers opportunities for growth and strengthened relationships. It requires patience, self-reflection, and a commitment to personal growth—qualities essential in overcoming narcissistic behaviors. Are you ready to change how you handle conflict and build stronger, healthier relationships?

CHAPTER 5
REINFORCING SELF-WORTH AND EMPATHY

DIFFERENTIATING NARCISSISTIC FROM HEALTHY SELF-ESTEEM

Self-esteem is the cornerstone of our identity, influencing how we relationships, face challenges, and perceive our place in the world. Yet, not all forms of self-esteem are created equal. Distinguishing between narcissistic self-esteem and healthy self-esteem is crucial for personal growth and genuine well-being. This differentiation sheds light on the pathways toward developing a self-view that's both resilient and rooted in reality.

- **Narcissistic Self-Esteem**: Characterized by an inflated sense of superiority and entitlement, narcissistic self-esteem is externally oriented. It depends heavily on validation from others, achievements, status, and the power one holds. This type of self-esteem is fragile, constantly needing external reinforcement to remain intact. It often leads to a cycle of seeking admiration and avoiding criticism at all costs, as any threat to this inflated self-view can trigger deep insecurities. Narcissistic self-esteem operates from

a place of scarcity and competition. It views success and acknowledgment as finite resources, where one person's gain is seen as another's loss. This zero-sum perspective on life can lead to relationships marred by jealousy, manipulation, and a lack of genuine connection.
- **Healthy Self-Esteem**: In contrast, healthy self-esteem is internally based. It stems from a deep sense of self-worth that is independent of external accomplishments, social status, or the approval of others. This form of self-esteem recognizes one's inherent value and embraces both strengths and vulnerabilities without the need for comparison or competition. Healthy self-esteem fosters a growth mindset. It allows individuals to view challenges as opportunities for learning and development, rather than threats to their self-image. It encourages empathy, both for oneself and others, and cultivates relationships built on mutual respect and understanding.
- **Building Healthy Self-Esteem**: The journey from narcissistic to healthy self-esteem begins with self-reflection and a commitment to inner work. It involves challenging long-held beliefs about worthiness and success, and gradually shifting the basis of self-esteem from external validation to internal acceptance. Practices such as mindfulness, self-compassion exercises, and cognitive-behavioral strategies can be instrumental in this transformation. Mindfulness helps bring awareness to the automatic thoughts and beliefs that underpin narcissistic self-esteem, allowing for a more objective evaluation of these patterns. Self-compassion offers a kinder, more forgiving approach to viewing oneself, counteracting the harsh self-criticism that often accompanies narcissistic self-esteem.
- **Empathy as a Bridge**: Empathy, both for oneself and others, plays a key role in developing healthy self-esteem. By understanding and connecting with the experiences of others, we begin to see that our struggles, insecurities, and imperfections are part of the shared human experience. This realization can diminish the need to

project an image of perfection or superiority, paving the way for more authentic and fulfilling relationships.

Continuing on the journey towards embracing a healthier self-esteem, understanding the key role of external validation—and learning to transcend its grasp—is essential. The quest for constant approval from others is a hallmark of narcissistic self-esteem, where one's value is perilously pegged to the shifting sands of public opinion, achievements, and recognition. This dependency creates a fragile sense of self that can easily crumble under criticism or failure.

- **Recognizing the Crux of the Issue**: At the core, the need for external validation stems from a deep-seated belief that one's worth is contingent upon others' perceptions. It's a relentless pursuit for a mirage of acceptance that, even when attained, never truly satisfies the thirst for genuine self-appreciation and respect.
- **Fostering Internal Validation**: The antidote to this dependency is cultivating an internal source of validation. This means learning to appreciate oneself for inherent qualities and actions rather than external achievements or accolades. It involves a shift from 'being good in the eyes of others' to 'feeling good about oneself,' irrespective of external judgments.
- **Self-Compassion as a Pathway**: One of the most powerful tools in this transformation is the practice of self-compassion. By treating oneself with the same kindness, understanding, and forgiveness one would offer a good friend, individuals can begin to dismantle the harsh self-criticism and conditional self-esteem that drives the need for external validation.
- **Embracing Imperfection**: Part of developing a healthy self-esteem involves embracing one's imperfections. Recognizing that

flawlessness is an unrealistic and unnecessary standard allows individuals to appreciate their unique qualities and contributions to the world, fostering a sense of self-worth that is resilient to external pressures.
- **Building Authentic Connections**: Overcoming the need for external validation opens the door to more authentic relationships. Freed from the compulsion to impress or compete for attention, individuals can form deeper connections based on mutual respect, empathy, and genuine interest in each other.
- **Setting Personal Goals**: Focusing on personal growth and setting intrinsic goals can also diminish the reliance on external validation. Pursuing interests and ambitions for the joy they bring, rather than for recognition, cultivates a sense of fulfillment and achievement that is self-sustaining.
- **Practical Steps Forward**: Encourage readers to reflect on moments when they sought external validation and to explore the feelings and beliefs underlying these instances. Suggest journaling exercises focused on gratitude for one's qualities and achievements, independent of external validation. Recommend mindfulness practices to stay present and reduce the impact of social comparison.

By navigating away from the need for external validation, individuals not only fortify their self-esteem but also pave the way for a life marked by authentic self-expression, deeper relationships, and a true sense of inner fulfillment. This chapter should serve as a sign for those looking to reclaim their self-worth from the shadows of external approval, guiding them towards a more self-compassionate, confident, and empathetic existence.

Cultivating a stable and positive self-view

Self-esteem is the cornerstone of our identity, influencing how we relate to others, face challenges, and perceive our place in the world. Yet, not all forms of self-esteem are created equal. Distinguishing between narcissistic self-esteem and healthy self-esteem is crucial for personal growth and genuine well-being. This differentiation sheds light on the pathways toward developing a self-view that's both resilient and rooted in reality.

Narcissistic self-esteem is characterized by an inflated sense of superiority and entitlement. It depends heavily on validation from others, achievements, status, and the power one holds. This type of self-esteem is fragile, constantly needing external reinforcement to remain intact. It often leads to a cycle of seeking admiration and avoiding criticism at all costs, as any threat to this inflated self-view can trigger deep insecurities. It operates from a place of scarcity and competition, viewing success and acknowledgment as finite resources, where one person's gain is seen as another's loss. This zero-sum perspective on life can lead to relationships marred by jealousy, manipulation, and a lack of genuine connection. In contrast, healthy self-esteem is internally based. It stems from a deep sense of self-worth that is independent of external accomplishments, social status, or the approval of others. This form of self-esteem recognizes one's inherent value and embraces both strengths and vulnerabilities without the need for comparison or competition. Healthy self-esteem fosters a growth mindset, allowing individuals to view challenges as opportunities for learning and development, rather than threats to their self-image. It encourages empathy, both for oneself and others, and cultivates relationships built on mutual respect and understanding. To start building healthy self-esteem, one must engage in self-reflection and commit to inner work. This means challenging long-held beliefs about worthiness and success and gradually shifting the basis of self-esteem from external validation to internal acceptance. Practices such as mindfulness, self-compassion exercises, and cognitive-behavioral strategies can be instrumental in this transformation. Mindfulness helps bring awareness to the automatic thoughts and beliefs that underpin narcissistic self-esteem, allowing for a more objective evaluation of these patterns. Self-compassion offers a kinder, more forgiving approach to viewing oneself, counteracting the harsh self-criticism that often accompanies narcissistic self-esteem.

Empathy, both for oneself and others, plays a key role in developing healthy self-esteem. By understanding and connecting with the experiences of others, we begin to see that our struggles, insecurities, and imperfections are part of the shared human experience. This realization can diminish the need to project an image of perfection or superiority, paving the way for more authentic and fulfilling relationships. Building healthy self-esteem also involves setting boundaries. It means learning to say no to situations or relationships that drain our self-worth and saying yes to those that nourish and support our inner well-being. Have you ever noticed how certain people or situations make you feel less valued? Recognizing these patterns is the first step in protecting your self-esteem.

As we continue to explore the facets of genuine self-esteem and empathy, remember that each step forward enriches not only our lives but the lives of those around us. Have you thought about how developing a stable and positive self-view can impact your relationships and overall happiness?

EMPATHY AS A PATHWAY TO CHANGE

Empathy, the ability to understand and share the feelings of another, is not just a trait some people are born with; it's a skill anyone can develop with practice. Let's explore daily practices that can help us become more empathetic, transforming our relationships and our own well-being.

Empathy starts with listening—really listening—not just waiting for your turn to speak. Have you ever noticed how much you miss when you're thinking about what to say next instead of focusing on the other person? Practicing active listening means paying full attention to the speaker, observing their body language, and reflecting on their words. This deep listening can make others feel truly heard and understood. Another way to build empathy is by being curious about other people's lives. Ask open-ended questions like, "How was your day?" or "What's been on your mind lately?" and show genuine interest in their answers. This helps you step into their shoes and see the world from their perspective, breaking down barriers of misunderstanding. Empathetic actions also have a powerful impact. Simple acts of kindness, like offering a comforting word or a helping hand, can make someone feel seen and valued.

Have you ever experienced a time when someone's small act of kindness brightened your day? These actions build trust and mend broken relationships, fostering a sense of community and understanding. Empathy can ripple outwards, inspiring others to act kindly as well. Imagine if every kind act you performed encouraged someone else to do the same. This chain reaction can transform families, communities, and even societies, creating a supportive environment where everyone feels understood and valued. To make empathy a part of your daily life, start by reflecting on your interactions. Did you listen more than you spoke? Did you show interest in others' feelings and experiences? Reflecting on these questions can help you identify areas for growth. Also, consider keeping a journal to jot down moments when you felt empathy or noticed a lack of it. This practice can highlight patterns and help you improve over time. Mindfulness is another tool that enhances empathy. Being present in the moment allows you to notice subtle emotional cues from others and respond with compassion. Try mindfulness exercises, like deep breathing or short meditation sessions, to stay grounded and aware throughout your day. Cultivating empathy isn't just about how we treat others; it's about changing our perspective. It challenges us to move beyond our own needs and concerns to a place of compassion and understanding. This shift enriches our relationships and enhances our own sense of peace and connection to the world.

Extending empathy beyond personal spheres

Extending empathy beyond our personal spheres into the broader community offers both a powerful opportunity for positive change and unique challenges. This extension requires us to empathize with people we may never meet, situations we may never experience, and issues far beyond our own lives. It's about understanding that our actions and attitudes can have far-reaching effects, cultivating a sense of global citizenship and interconnectedness.

One significant challenge is overcoming our natural tendency to empathize more easily with those who are similar to us or with whom we share a direct connection. This "empathy gap" makes it hard to fully understand and care about the struggles of people from different backgrounds, cultures, or experiences. How can we bridge this gap? Actively educating ourselves about others' lives and perspectives is crucial. Seek out stories and information that broaden your understanding and challenge your preconceptions. Have you ever tried reading a book or watching a documentary about a culture different from your own? Another challenge is the overwhelming nature of global issues like poverty, inequality, and climate change. These problems can make individual efforts feel insignificant. However, empathy can drive collective action. By joining others who share our concerns, we can amplify our impact and contribute to larger movements for change. Think about how powerful it is when communities come together to address a common issue—each small action adds up to significant progress. Practically, extending empathy involves engaging with our communities, volunteering, and supporting causes that address systemic issues. It means using our voices, votes, and resources to advocate for policies and practices that uplift the most vulnerable among us. It also involves listening—truly listening—to those directly affected by these issues. How often do we take the time to really hear the stories of people impacted by poverty, discrimination, or environmental degradation? To overcome the challenges of developing empathy on a larger scale, we must commit to seeing the world through a lens of compassion and interconnectedness. This requires patience, as changing deeply ingrained attitudes and behaviors can be a slow process. It also necessitates humility, recognizing that we all have biases and gaps in our understanding, and that there is always more to learn. The transformative power of empathy, when extended beyond our immediate circles, lies in its ability to break down barriers, foster a deeper sense of global community, and inspire actions that contribute to a more equitable and compassionate world. Imagine a world where empathy guides our decisions and actions, where we consider the impact of our choices on people across the globe. One practical step to enhance empathy is to get involved in local community projects. Volunteering at a food bank, participating in neighborhood clean-ups, or mentoring youth can provide direct experiences that expand our empathy. These activities connect us with people from different walks of life, helping us understand their challenges and strengths. Supporting global causes is another way to extend empathy. Consider donating to international charities, participating in awareness campaigns, or advocating for global issues on social media. Your actions can make a difference, no matter how small they may seem. Have you ever thought about how your contributions, even if modest, can create ripples of positive change?

Listening to diverse voices is also essential. Follow blogs, podcasts, and social media accounts of people from different backgrounds. Engage in conversations that broaden your perspective. Remember, empathy starts with understanding, and understanding begins with listening.

SUSTAINING PERSONAL GROWTH

Sustaining personal growth is like tending to a garden; it requires continuous care, periodic assessment, and the willingness to adapt and evolve. The journey of self-improvement is never linear, nor is it finite. It's an ongoing process that demands dedication, self-awareness, and the courage to confront our limitations and move beyond them. In this chapter, we'll explore the fundamental principles that support long-term strategies for self-improvement and underscore the critical importance of continuous self-reflection in this endeavor.

At the heart of sustained personal growth is the commitment to lifelong learning and the openness to new experiences. Embracing curiosity and allowing it to lead us toward new challenges, skills, and understandings is essential. It involves setting aside the fear of failure and recognizing that every setback is a stepping stone towards greater understanding and resilience. How often do we avoid trying something new because we fear not succeeding right away? Continuous self-reflection acts as the compass guiding this journey. Regularly taking stock of our actions, decisions, and their outcomes allows us to identify patterns in our behavior, both constructive and detrimental. By questioning why we react in certain ways and whether those reactions serve our highest good, we gain the insight needed to modify our path forward. Have you ever paused to consider why you respond a certain way to criticism or praise?

One practical strategy for embedding continuous self-reflection into our lives is maintaining a reflection journal. This isn't just a diary of events but a tool for probing deeper into our psyche. In it, we ask ourselves hard questions, celebrate our successes, and honestly evaluate areas where we fell short of our expectations. This habit fosters self-awareness and serves as a historical record of our growth over time. How often do we take the time to reflect on our day and what we learned from it? Seeking feedback from those we trust is another long-term strategy for self-improvement. While self-reflection provides internal insights, external perspectives can highlight blind spots in our self-perception. Constructive feedback, when received with openness and humility, can be incredibly transformative. Have you ever asked a close friend or mentor for their honest opinion about your actions and attitudes? Embedding the practice of gratitude into our daily routine can significantly bolster our journey towards sustained growth. Gratitude shifts our focus from what we lack to what we possess, from our failures to our progress. It cultivates a positive mindset conducive to growth and resilience. Can you recall a moment today when you felt genuinely grateful for something or someone? In cultivating a stable and positive self-view, it's crucial to distinguish between self-compassion and self-indulgence. Self-compassion means treating ourselves with the same kindness and understanding we'd offer a good friend. It means acknowledging our faults while also recognizing our inherent worth and potential. This balanced self-view encourages us to strive for better, not from a place of inadequacy, but from a desire to fulfill our potential. Do you treat yourself with the same kindness you offer to others? To sustain personal growth, we must also learn to be comfortable with discomfort. Growth often requires stepping out of our comfort zones and facing the unknown. By learning to tolerate discomfort, we build the resilience necessary to tackle new challenges and seize opportunities for development. When was the last time you stepped out of your comfort zone and learned something valuable? Sustaining personal growth is a deliberate and lifelong pursuit. It requires a commitment to continuous learning, self-reflection, and the cultivation of a positive and resilient mindset. Each day offers a new opportunity for growth, learning, and transformation. Are you ready to embrace the ongoing adventure of self-improvement? Let's continue to reflect, learn, and grow, always remembering that the journey itself is just as important as the destination. Moving away from narcissistic behaviors towards a life enriched with empathy and self-worth, support networks and professional therapy play key roles. These resources are not just crutches in times of vulnerability but also powerful tools that guide, educate, and empower us to foster and maintain lasting change.

Utilizing support networks, whether they consist of friends, family, or groups dedicated to personal growth, is essential for maintaining momentum in our journey. These networks remind us that we're not alone in our struggles. They provide a sounding board for our thoughts and feelings, reflecting both our progress and areas that still need attention. Engaging with individuals who share similar goals or have navigated similar paths can bolster our motivation and resilience. Have you ever noticed how much easier it is to face challenges when you know someone else understands what you're going through? Support networks offer shared experiences that highlight the common humanity in our struggles, reducing feelings of shame or isolation often associated with narcissistic tendencies. This sense of connection can be incredibly grounding. When we hear others share their stories of overcoming similar issues, it gives us hope and practical insights for our journey. Can you think of a time when a friend's advice or support made a significant difference in your life? On the other hand, professional therapy offers a structured and insightful approach to understanding and changing deep-seated patterns of narcissistic behavior. Therapists trained in dealing with narcissism can provide strategies tailored to individual needs, helping to unravel the complex network of behaviors and thoughts that sustain these patterns. Therapy offers a safe space to explore the roots of our actions and reactions, including those stemming from childhood experiences or trauma. How often do we take the time to dig deep into the reasons behind our behaviors? Preventing relapse into old narcissistic patterns requires conscious and continuous effort. One effective strategy is to establish and regularly revisit clear, realistic goals for personal growth. These goals serve as benchmarks that keep us aligned with our values and the vision of who we aspire to be. Have you set specific goals for your personal growth, and how often do you check in on your progress? Developing a mindfulness practice is another crucial aspect. Mindfulness keeps us anchored in the present, enabling us to observe our thoughts and feelings without judgment. This awareness is key to recognizing the early signs of potential relapse, such as resorting to old defense mechanisms or patterns of manipulation and control. Do you practice mindfulness, and if so, how has it helped you stay grounded? Maintaining a habit of regular self-reflection is essential. This can be facilitated through journaling, meditation, or therapy sessions. Reflection allows us to assess our progress, celebrate our successes, and identify areas that require more work. It's through this ongoing process of self-examination that we can catch and correct course whenever we find ourselves slipping back into old patterns. When was the last time you took a moment to reflect on your day and your actions?

Moving away from narcissistic behaviors towards a life enriched with empathy and self-worth, support networks and professional therapy play key roles. These resources are not just crutches in times of vulnerability but also powerful tools that guide, educate, and empower us to foster and maintain lasting change. They help us see that our efforts are worthwhile and that we are capable of creating meaningful, positive transformations in our lives.

CHAPTER 6
ENHANCING INTERPERSONAL RELATIONSHIPS

SHIFTING FOCUS TO OTHERS

From Me to We: Changing the Dynamics

In the journey toward self-improvement, shifting from a self-centered mindset to a more inclusive, empathetic lifestyle requires a fundamental change in perspective. This transition from 'me' to 'we' isn't about losing one's identity but expanding it to include others meaningfully. It's about changing how we perceive ourselves and our relationships with those around us.

A key aspect of narcissism is an excessive focus on oneself, often to the detriment of others. This isn't just about being selfish or egotistical but involves a deep-rooted drive to place oneself at the center of everything. This can lead to disregarding the feelings and needs of others and failing to understand their perspectives. Recognizing this tendency and its negative impact is the first step toward change. However, recognizing the need for change is just the beginning. Implementing this change in daily life requires consistent effort and practice. It means consciously choosing to listen to others, empathize with their feelings, and consider their needs and desires. It means stepping outside our comfort zone and making an effort to connect with others on a deeper level. Think about how often we listen to others just to reply rather than to understand. What would happen if we truly listened? This might mean asking others about their day and genuinely listening to their responses, rather than simply waiting for our turn to speak. It might mean acknowledging when we are wrong and apologizing sincerely, rather than defending our actions or shifting the blame. It might mean offering help or support to others, not for the sake of recognition or reward, but simply because it's the right thing to do. This shift from 'me' to 'we' also involves changing how we perceive success and worth. In a narcissistic mindset, success is often defined in terms of personal achievement and recognition. However, in a more inclusive mindset, success can also be defined by our positive impact on others and our contributions to the community. This can lead to a more fulfilling and meaningful life as we begin to recognize the value of our relationships and connections with others. Imagine redefining success in terms of the positive changes we bring to our community. Changing the dynamics in this way is not a quick or easy process. It requires a willingness to confront our flaws and weaknesses and the courage to change our behaviors and attitudes. It may involve seeking professional help, such as therapy or counseling, to gain a deeper understanding of our narcissistic tendencies and how to overcome them. It may also involve practicing mindfulness and empathy to help us become more aware of our thoughts and feelings and more attuned to the needs and feelings of others. The journey from 'me' to 'we' involves recognizing the need for change, implementing this change in our daily lives, and redefining our perceptions of success and worth. While this journey may be challenging, the rewards—in terms of improved relationships, increased empathy, and a more fulfilling life—are well worth the effort. By fostering a more inclusive and empathetic outlook, we not only enrich our own lives but also contribute to a more connected and compassionate world.

Consider how this shift can transform your relationships and overall life satisfaction. Let's explore the steps you can take to make this important change.

Practical Examples of Empathetic vs. Narcissistic Communication

Understanding the dynamics of empathetic versus narcissistic communication can significantly enhance your interpersonal relationships. Here are practical examples to illustrate the difference between the two, helping you navigate your interactions more mindfully.

Example 1: Responding to a Partner's Concerns

Narcissistic Communication: Your partner expresses feeling neglected lately due to your busy schedule. You immediately retort, "You know how important my work is. Why can't you see that? You're just adding to my stress."

Empathetic Communication: You listen quietly, acknowledging their feelings, "I see you're feeling left out because of my focus on work. Let's find a way to spend more quality time together."

Insight

Empathetic communication involves listening and validating the other person's feelings, while narcissistic communication dismisses them and prioritizes self-interest.

Example 2: Handling Criticism

Narcissistic Communication: A colleague suggests an improvement to your project proposal. You snap back, "I know what I'm doing. Maybe you should focus on your work."

Empathetic Communication: You consider the feedback thoughtfully, "Thank you for the input. I hadn't considered that perspective. Let's discuss how we can integrate these ideas."

Insight

Embracing constructive criticism with an open mind and a willingness to grow is a hallmark of empathetic communication.

Example 3: Expressing Needs and Boundaries

Narcissistic Communication: You need some alone time and say, "I'm taking the day off. I can't deal with anyone today, your needs included."

Empathetic Communication: You communicate your need for space in a considerate way, "I'm feeling a bit overwhelmed and need some quiet time to recharge. Let's plan something enjoyable together tomorrow."

Insight

Empathetic communication respects both your needs and those of others, finding a balance that honors both.

Example 4: Sharing Successes

Narcissistic Communication: After receiving a promotion, you boast, "I'm obviously the best choice. It was only a matter of time before they recognized my superiority."

Empathetic Communication: When sharing your success, you include others, "I'm really excited about the promotion. I couldn't have achieved this without the support and hard work of my team."

Insight

Acknowledging the role of others in your successes fosters goodwill and respect, a core aspect of empathetic communication.

Implementing Empathetic Communication

- **Active Listening**: Truly hear what the other person is saying, without formulating your response while they speak.
- **Validation**: Acknowledge the feelings and perspectives of others, even if you don't agree.
- **Self-Reflection**: Before responding, consider the impact of your words and actions on the other person.
- Inclusive Language: Use "we" and "us" to foster a sense of teamwork and unity.

Empathetic communication brings up relationships by ensuring all parties feel heard, valued, and respected. By choosing empathy over narcissism in your interactions, you not only improve your relationships but also encourage personal growth and understanding. This chapter aims to guide you in recognizing the moments when you can shift from self-focused to others-focused communication, deepening your connections and enhancing your interpersonal dynamics.

Why Falling Back Isn't Failing

When we face setbacks, it can feel like the end of our progress. It's easy to doubt ourselves, especially when we're working hard to change old habits and behaviors. But falling back into old patterns isn't failing; it's part of the process.

Life isn't a straight path. It's full of twists and turns, ups and downs. This means that even when you fall back into narcissistic tendencies, it doesn't mean you've failed. It's just a bump in the road, an opportunity to learn and grow. Think about a time when you slipped back into an old habit. Instead of seeing it as a failure, can you see it as a chance to learn something new about yourself? Maybe you fell back into old patterns because you were stressed or tired. Understanding why it happened can help you avoid the same triggers next time. Overcoming narcissism is a long journey. It's not something you can change overnight. These behaviors are deeply ingrained, often built over many years. It takes time to unlearn these ways and replace them with healthier habits.

When you're stressed or feel threatened, it's easy to revert to old behaviors. But it's important to be kind to yourself in these moments. Instead of getting angry with yourself, try to observe what happened. What triggered this behavior? What can you do differently next time?

Remember, every setback is a setup for a comeback. Each time you fall back, you learn something new about yourself. You learn about your triggers, your strengths, and your areas for improvement. You learn what works for you and what doesn't. Consider this: how do you respond when you fall back? Do you get stuck in self-criticism, or do you pick yourself up and keep going? It's not about never falling back; it's about how you handle it when you do. Each time you fall back, you have the chance to respond with resilience and determination. You're not failing; you're learning. You're growing. You're writing a new chapter in your journey toward overcoming narcissism. So, when you stumble, don't be too hard on yourself. Instead, see it as a chance to learn and grow. Embrace the setback, learn from it, and use it to become a better version of yourself. Remember, the journey to self-improvement isn't about perfection; it's about progress. Think about how you can use setbacks to your advantage. How can you learn from them and continue to move forward? Each stumble is a step toward understanding and growth.

In the end, falling back isn't failing. It's a part of your journey toward becoming a healthier, more empathetic person. Embrace it, learn from it, and keep moving forward.

. . .

How to Bounce Back Stronger

In the journey of self-improvement and growth, resilience is a paramount virtue. It is the ability to bounce back stronger, to rise again after a setback, and to renew oneself continually. As we dive into this aspect of transformation, let's remember that moving away from narcissistic tendencies is not about self-deprecation but about self-evolution.

The first step towards bouncing back stronger is embracing humility. Humility is the antithesis of narcissism. It is the understanding that we are not the center of the universe; we are part of a larger, interconnected net of life. This realization helps in maintaining a healthy perspective, thereby fostering resilience. It enables us to view setbacks not as personal failures but as opportunities for growth and learning.

Secondly, cultivating self-awareness is key to resilience. Being aware of our emotions, thought patterns, and behaviors can help us recognize when we are slipping back into narcissistic tendencies. It makes us conscious of our actions and their impact on others. This awareness can be a potent tool in mitigating the adverse effects of narcissism, helping us recover faster and emerge stronger.

Moreover, the ability to empathize with others plays a vital role in overcoming narcissism. Empathy allows us to understand other people's feelings and perspectives and to respond with kindness and understanding. It helps us to see beyond our desires and needs, thereby promoting healthier relationships. When we are empathetic, we are more likely to acknowledge our mistakes, apologize, and make amends, which in turn, helps us bounce back stronger from setbacks.

It's also crucial to practice self-compassion. Many narcissists are harsh and critical of themselves, which only perpetuates their narcissistic behavior. By being kind to ourselves, we can heal the wounds that often underlie narcissism. Self-compassion involves acknowledging our imperfections, forgiving ourselves for our mistakes, and treating ourselves with the same kindness we would offer a friend. This kind of self-love can help us recover from setbacks and grow stronger.

Finally, developing a growth mindset is integral to bouncing back stronger. A growth mindset is the belief that our abilities and intelligence can be developed through dedication and hard work. It's the opposite of a fixed mindset, which assumes that our traits are fixed and unchangeable. With a growth mindset, we view challenges as opportunities to grow, not as threats to our self-worth. We learn to appreciate the process of struggle and growth instead of focusing solely on the end result. This shift in perspective can be incredibly empowering in overcoming narcissism.

In conclusion, bouncing back stronger from narcissism involves embodying humility, cultivating self-awareness and empathy, practicing self-compassion, and adopting a growth mindset. These qualities not only help us recover from setbacks but also foster personal growth and self-improvement. The journey from narcissism to a healthier self is not an easy one, but with resilience, it is certainly possible. Remember, it's not about being perfect; it's about being better than you were yesterday.

EMPATHETIC COMMUNICATION

Acknowledging the Courage to Change

Changing how we act, especially if we've been self-centered, takes a lot of bravery. Admitting that we need to change can be one of the hardest steps because it means accepting that we haven't always been our best selves. This is not about blaming ourselves but about understanding and moving forward.

Have you ever felt that you're more focused on your own needs than others' feelings? Realizing that we might have been selfish or used others to feel good about ourselves can make us feel guilty. But this guilt means we're starting to care about how our actions affect others, which is a good sign. Imagine a time when you might have hurt someone without meaning to. How did you feel when you realized it? Feeling uncomfortable is part of growing. It shows that you're starting to see things from other people's perspectives. This awareness is the first step toward making real changes. Changing these habits isn't something that happens overnight. It's a continuous process where we need to keep reflecting on our actions and their impact. Think about your daily interactions. Are you genuinely listening to others, or are you waiting for your turn to talk? Active listening is a powerful way to show empathy and understand others better. When was the last time you admitted you were wrong? Practicing humility is another important step. It's okay not to have all the answers. Acknowledging our mistakes can help us grow and improve our relationships. Giving sincere compliments can also make a big difference. Not only does it make others feel good, but it also helps us to focus on others' positive qualities.Changing from being self-centered to more empathetic and caring isn't easy. It takes consistent effort and patience. There will be times when you slip back into old habits, and that's okay. What's important is how you respond to these setbacks. Do you give up, or do you learn from them and keep trying? Think about a time when you felt vulnerable. How did that experience help you connect with others? Vulnerability isn't a weakness. It's a way to build deeper connections because it shows that we are human and that we care. Being open and honest about our struggles can help others feel comfortable doing the same. Every step you take towards change, no matter how small, is progress. It's not about becoming perfect but about becoming a better version of yourself. Remember, you're not alone in this journey. Everyone is learning and growing, and every bit of effort counts.

Can you recall a recent interaction where you put someone else's needs before your own? How did it make you feel? Focusing on others doesn't mean you neglect yourself. It means you value others' feelings and needs as much as your own, which leads to more meaningful relationships.

So, let's celebrate the courage it takes to change. It's okay to make mistakes and feel vulnerable. These are signs of growth and progress. With each step, you're not just improving your own life but also positively impacting the lives of those around you. Here's to embracing change and becoming the best version of yourself.

The Art of Active Listening: Why Your Words Matter Less Than You Think

You might find it surprising, but one of the most potent tools in combating narcissism is Learning to listen actively is one of the most powerful steps in moving away from self-centered behavior. Active listening means truly focusing on what the other person is saying, understanding their feelings, and showing that you care about their perspective. It's not just about hearing the words but grasping the emotions and intentions behind them.

Have you ever found yourself thinking about what you want to say next while someone else is talking? This is a common habit, especially for those who are used to being the center of attention. Narcissism often makes us focus on our own thoughts and needs, but this can create a barrier between us and others, making them feel ignored and undervalued.

What if we could change this? Instead of always thinking about our own responses, what if we tried to understand the other person's point of view? Active listening can help bridge the gap between us and others. It means paying full attention to the speaker, putting away distractions, and really trying to understand their message. This simple yet powerful practice can help us become more empathetic and connected. Active listening involves a few key steps. First, make a conscious effort to listen without interrupting. This shows respect and allows the speaker to feel heard. Maintain eye contact and nod to show that you are engaged. Ask open-ended questions to encourage the speaker to share more about their thoughts and feelings. Repeat back what you've heard to ensure you've understood correctly and to show that you are paying attention. Why does this matter? When people feel listened to, they feel valued. This can help strengthen relationships and build trust. It also helps us to understand different perspectives and experiences, which can reduce our own biases and judgments. By listening actively, we learn to step out of our own bubble and see the world through others' eyes. Think about the last conversation you had. Were you really listening, or were you more focused on your own thoughts? By practicing active listening, we can start to change our interactions and become more empathetic. It's not about agreeing with everything the other person says but about understanding their point of view and showing that it matters. Active listening is not a quick fix but a life-long practice. It requires patience and persistence. The more we practice, the better we become at it. This practice can help us unlearn old habits of interrupting or dominating conversations and relearn how to engage in a more meaningful way. Imagine a world where everyone felt truly heard and understood. Active listening can help us move towards that world. It helps us connect on a deeper level, building stronger relationships and fostering a sense of community. When we listen with empathy, we show that we care about others' feelings and experiences, which can lead to greater mutual respect and understanding.

So, let's commit to listening more actively. Let's put aside our own thoughts and truly focus on others. This small change can have a big impact on our relationships and our personal growth. By listening with our hearts, we can become more empathetic, reduce our narcissistic tendencies, and create a more compassionate world.

Practical Exercises to Improve Listening Skills

As we dive deeper into the journey of transformation from narcissism, we encounter the crucial aspect of honing our listening skills. The path to self-improvement necessitates the cultivation of active listening, which can be achieved through practical exercises designed to challenge our default patterns and attitudes.

1. **Exercise one**: Mindful listening. This exercise draws from mindfulness practices, encouraging you to be fully present and attentive in your conversations. It requires you to quiet your mind, letting go of the constant chatter that often distracts us, and truly focus on the words being spoken to you. Do not interrupt or formulate responses while the other person is still speaking. Instead, truly listen, absorb, and reflect on their words before responding. This exercise will help you understand the importance of giving others the space to express themselves.
2. **Exercise two**: The echo technique. This technique involves repeating or paraphrasing what the speaker has said, which not only demonstrates that you were listening but also gives you a chance to ensure your understanding is correct. This practice can be uncomfortable for some, as it requires suppressing the urge to interject with your own thoughts and opinions. However, with

time and practice, it can significantly improve your listening skills and empathy.
3. **Exercise three**: Ask for clarification. This is a simple yet effective method to improve listening skills. By asking for clarification, you show the speaker that you are interested in understanding their point of view. This can be as simple as asking, "Could you elaborate on that?" or "What do you mean by that?" This encourages a deeper level of conversation and allows you to better comprehend the other person's perspective.
4. **Exercise four**: Non-verbal cues. This exercise involves paying attention to non-verbal cues such as body language, facial expressions, and tone of voice. These cues can provide a wealth of information about what the speaker is feeling, allowing you to respond more empathetically. This exercise not only improves your listening skills but also enhances your overall communication skills.
5. **Exercise five**: Practice silence. This might be the hardest exercise for someone with narcissistic tendencies. The aim here is to practice being comfortable with silence in a conversation. Resist the urge to fill every pause or silence with your own words. Allow the other person to take their time to express their thoughts. This exercise teaches patience and respect for other people's conversational rhythms.

As you engage in these exercises, remember that progress may be slow and incremental. You might find them challenging, especially if you're used to dominating conversations. However, the rewards are immense. Improved listening skills can lead to deeper, more meaningful relationships, and a greater understanding of others.

As a recovering narcissist, cultivating your listening skills is a crucial step towards becoming more empathetic and less self-centered. These practical exercises are designed to challenge the habits that have reinforced your narcissistic tendencies, and replace them with healthier, more respectful communication patterns. Remember, the path to change is a journey, not a destination. With patience, practice, and persistence, you can transform the way you interact with the world.

SETTING HEALTHY BOUNDARIES

Understanding the Importance of Personal Boundaries

Understanding the importance of personal boundaries is crucial for maintaining healthy relationships and a strong sense of self. Boundaries are like invisible lines that define where you end and someone else begins. They protect your emotional well-being and help you interact with others in a respectful and meaningful way. Sometimes people think boundaries are like walls that keep others out. But really, they're more like guidelines that show others how you want to be treated. They reflect your values, your limits, and your respect for yourself. Have you ever felt upset because you did something you didn't want to do, just to please someone else? Or stayed quiet when you really wanted to speak up? These feelings often come from having unclear or weak boundaries. Setting healthy boundaries starts with understanding your own needs and feelings. It's about having an honest conversation with yourself. What makes you uncomfortable? What do you need to feel respected? This inner dialogue helps you realize that it's okay to say no, to ask for space, and to speak up for yourself. At the heart of setting boundaries is the belief that you deserve to be treated with respect and kindness. It means recognizing that your needs are important, your feelings are valid, and you have the right to protect your personal space. This understanding transforms self-doubt into self-confidence. Setting boundaries is not a one-time thing; it's a continuous process. Every day, you make choices about how to spend your time, who you interact with, and how you respond to others' demands. Sometimes, you might need to rethink your relationships and set new limits. This can be uncomfortable, especially if people are used to you always saying yes. But with time and practice, it gets easier. When you start to set boundaries, you'll notice positive changes. Your relationships will become more genuine because they'll be based on mutual respect.

You'll feel freer, as you won't always feel pressured to make others happy at your own expense. To set boundaries, start by clearly defining what you need and what you won't accept. Practice saying no in a kind but firm way. Remember, it's okay to put yourself first. You might say something like, "I appreciate your invitation, but I need some time for myself," or "I understand your point, but I feel differently about this."

As you continue to practice setting boundaries, you'll find it becomes more natural. You'll feel more empowered and less stressed, knowing you have the right to protect your well-being. It's important to remember that setting boundaries doesn't mean you're being selfish. It means you're taking care of yourself, which allows you to be more present and supportive for others.

Communicating Boundaries Clearly and Effectively

Communicating boundaries clearly and effectively is essential for healthy relationships. It's about explaining your limits in a way that others can understand and respect, making sure you protect your emotional well-being. How do you know where your boundaries lie? Think about what makes you comfortable and what doesn't. These boundaries can range from needing privacy to how you want to be treated during disagreements. Once you know your boundaries, you need to express them calmly and confidently. The way you speak—your tone, words, and timing—can make a big difference. Use "I" statements to focus on your feelings instead of "you" statements that might seem like you're blaming the other person. For instance, saying "I feel overwhelmed when I don't have time to myself in the evenings" is more effective than "You always take up all my time." Try rehearsing what you want to say ahead of time. Think about how the other person might respond and prepare for those reactions. This way, you'll feel more composed during the actual conversation, even if it gets tough. Remember that setting boundaries isn't a one-time event. Relationships change, and so might your boundaries. Keep talking with loved ones about your boundaries to make sure they understand and respect them. Regular check-ins can help reinforce your limits and allow for adjustments if needed. If you set a boundary, stick to it. If you waver, it can confuse others and undermine your efforts. Stand firm in your convictions, and don't let guilt or pressure make you change your mind.

Empathy plays an important role in this process too. Understand that others have their own needs and boundaries. Respecting their boundaries helps build a mutual understanding and strengthens your relationships. Clear communication of boundaries is crucial for self-care and healthy interactions. As we move forward, we'll explore how to maintain these boundaries and handle challenges when they arise. Every step you take to assert your boundaries helps you grow into a stronger, more confident person.

Think of this journey as a seed growing into a tree. With each step, your ability to assert your boundaries will grow, standing tall in the soil of self-respect and personal dignity.

Respecting the Boundaries of Others

Just as we assert our own boundaries to protect our well-being, respecting the boundaries of others is a testament to our maturity and empathy. It's about recognizing that everyone has their limits, their safe spaces that need to be acknowledged and honored. To the rich tapestry of human relationships, we must learn to discern and respect these invisible lines that others draw around their comfort zones.

Respecting boundaries is not merely a courteous nod to social norms; it is a deep acknowledgment of another's autonomy and a crucial component of trust. When we respect others' boundaries, we communicate that we value their feelings, their needs, and their right to personal space. It's a reciprocal dance — as we hope our boundaries to be respected, we must extend the same courtesy to those around us.

How, then, do we ensure we are respecting the boundaries of others? It starts with active listening and observation. Pay attention to verbal and non-verbal cues that signal comfort or discomfort. If someone seems hesitant or withdraws during a conversation, it may indicate that a boundary is being approached. Respect these signs without needing explicit statements or justifications.

Engage in open dialogue about boundaries. Encourage friends, family, and colleagues to express their limits and listen without judgment. When someone tells you their boundaries, honor them. Avoid the temptation to test or challenge these limits; such actions can erode trust and harm the relationship.

Understanding that boundaries can vary greatly from person to person is crucial. What may be a non-issue for one could be a significant boundary for another. This variance requires sensitivity and adaptability. It's about customizing your approach to each individual, fostering relationships where everyone involved feels understood and respected.

It's also important to remember that boundaries can change. Just as we grow and evolve, so do our comfort levels and needs. Check-ins can be a valuable way of ensuring that we are up to date with others' boundaries. This not only shows respect but also strengthens the relationship through ongoing communication and care.

Lastly, respecting boundaries means apologizing if we inadvertently cross them. It's about taking responsibility, acknowledging the impact of our actions, and striving to do better in the future. It reflects a commitment to the health of the relationship and the well-being of those we care about.

In our journey of transformation, just as a tree's roots must respect the space of others to coexist harmoniously, we too must learn the delicate art of respecting boundaries. As we progress, we will explore how to rebuild when boundaries are breached, how to reinforce them, and how to deal with the complexities of interpersonal dynamics with grace and empathy.

Are you ready to deepen your respect for the boundaries of others and, in doing so, enhance the quality of your relationships? The next section will guide you further into developing this essential skill, one that is important for your growth and for taking care of lasting, healthy connections.

Managing Violations Constructively

Even in the best relationships, sometimes boundaries get crossed. When this happens, it can feel really tough, but it's also a chance to learn and grow. Handling these situations well helps us keep our boundaries strong while staying close to those we care about. When someone crosses your boundary, it's normal to feel angry, hurt, or disappointed. But before you react, take a moment to pause. This pause helps you think clearly instead of reacting with strong emotions. Remember, the goal isn't to punish but to talk things out and help each other understand better. After taking a moment, talk to the person who crossed your boundary. Tell them calmly and clearly what happened and how it made you feel. Use "I" statements to explain your feelings without blaming them. For example, say, "I felt hurt when you told my secret without asking me. I really value privacy and need to feel safe sharing things with you."

As we said many times, listening is just as important as talking. Give the other person a chance to explain. Sometimes, boundaries get crossed because of misunderstandings, not because someone meant to hurt you. Talking things through can help both of you understand each other better. Sometimes, you need to set consequences if someone keeps crossing your boundaries. Consequences aren't about getting back at someone; they're about taking care of yourself. Make sure the consequences are fair and related to the boundary. For example, if someone keeps interrupting you, a consequence might be taking a break from talking to them when they do. It's also good to think about your boundary. Was it clear to the other person? Is it fair and realistic? Maybe the boundary wasn't explained well, or it needs to be adjusted. Reflecting on this can help you set better boundaries in the future.

Forgiveness is another important part. Forgiving doesn't mean you forget what happened or remove the boundary. It means letting go of the anger so it doesn't affect your relationship. Forgiving and talking things out can make your relationship stronger because you build more trust and respect for each other. Remember, handling boundary issues is a skill that takes practice. Be patient with yourself and others. Boundaries are something we constantly work on in our relationships. Each time you handle a boundary issue, you learn more about what you need, how to talk about it, and how to stay true to yourself even when things get tough.

As we keep learning about ourselves and our relationships, we'll explore more about how to communicate better and handle conflicts with grace and confidence.

CHAPTER 7
ADVANCED STRATEGIES FOR PERSONAL DEVELOPMENT

MASTERING EMOTIONAL REGULATION

Mastering emotional regulation is a cornerstone of personal development, especially for individuals working to overcome narcissistic tendencies. Emotional dysregulation often underpins narcissistic behaviors, leading to intense reactions to criticism, failure, or perceived slights. Recognizing and managing these emotions is not just about self-control; it's about deepening self-understanding and fostering genuine connections with others.

Techniques for Managing Intense Emotions

- Deep Breathing: When overwhelmed by intense emotions, take a moment to focus on your breath. Deep, slow breathing can help calm the nervous system and provide a pause to evaluate your feelings more clearly.
- Mindfulness Meditation: Regular practice of mindfulness meditation can increase your awareness of emotional triggers and reactions. It teaches you to observe your emotions without

judgment, understanding them as transient states rather than defining truths.
- Cognitive Reframing: Challenge and change the narratives you tell yourself about your emotions. For example, instead of thinking, "I must be admired to be valued," reframe it to, "My self-worth is inherent, not dependent on external validation."

The Role of Emotional Dysregulation in Narcissistic Behavior

Emotional dysregulation often manifests in narcissistic behaviors as a defense mechanism against feelings of vulnerability or inadequacy. It can lead to aggressive responses to criticism, a relentless pursuit of admiration, and difficulties in empathizing with others. By mastering emotional regulation, individuals can start to respond rather than react, reducing the need for these defensive behaviors.

Addressing emotional dysregulation involves acknowledging the discomfort of vulnerability and working through it. It requires a willingness to face the fears and insecurities that drive narcissistic behaviors, fostering a more authentic and empathetic approach to interactions.

Integrating Emotional Regulation into Daily Life

Incorporating emotional regulation into daily life is a practice that requires consistency and patience. It involves:

- Regularly practicing the techniques outlined, making them part of your routine.
- Seeking feedback from trusted individuals who can offer insights into your emotional responses and progress.
- Reflecting on instances of emotional dysregulation to understand their triggers and effects.

The Path Forward

Embracing emotional regulation is a powerful step towards overcoming narcissism. It enables a shift from a self-centered worldview to one that values and respects the emotions and needs of others. This journey, while challenging, is immensely rewarding, paving the way for more meaningful and satisfying relationships.

As we continue to explore advanced strategies for personal development, remember that each step taken towards mastering emotional regulation is a step towards a more balanced, empathetic, and fulfilling life. Are you ready to continue on this transformative journey, embracing the challenges and opportunities it presents? The next chapter awaits, filled with more strategies and insights to guide you on this path to personal growth.

Strategies for achieving emotional balance

Achieving emotional balance is a crucial aspect of personal development, especially for individuals working to overcome narcissistic behaviors. Emotional balance is the state where one can manage emotions effectively, without being overwhelmed by them or suppressing them. It involves recognizing emotions as they arise, understanding their source, and responding to them in a way that is healthy and constructive. Here are some strategies to help achieve emotional balance:

- **Mindfulness Practice**: Mindfulness is the practice of being present and fully engaged with whatever we are doing at the moment, without distraction or judgment. By practicing mindfulness, individuals can learn to observe their emotions without being controlled by them. This can involve mindfulness meditation, where one focuses on their breath or bodily sensations, allowing thoughts and feelings to come and go without attachment.
- **Emotional Literacy**: This involves developing the ability to recognize and name emotions accurately. Many times, people may

feel overwhelmed because they do not understand what they are feeling. By learning to identify and label emotions correctly, individuals can take the first step in managing them effectively.
- **Emotion Regulation Techniques**: Techniques such as deep breathing, progressive muscle relaxation, or visualization can help calm the nervous system and bring emotions into balance. These techniques can be particularly useful in moments of intense emotional distress.
- **Cognitive Restructuring**: This cognitive-behavioral therapy technique involves identifying and challenging negative thought patterns that can fuel emotional imbalance. By replacing these thoughts with more balanced and constructive ones, individuals can reduce emotional distress and develop a more positive outlook.
- **Healthy Expression of Emotions**: Finding constructive ways to express emotions can greatly contribute to emotional balance. This might involve communicating feelings in a clear and assertive manner, engaging in creative activities like writing or art, or participating in physical activities that help release emotional tension.
- **Building Emotional Resilience**: This involves developing coping strategies to deal with setbacks and challenges without resorting to narcissistic defenses. Resilience can be built through practices such as gratitude journaling, fostering positive relationships, and setting realistic goals.
- **Seeking Professional Help**: Sometimes, achieving emotional balance may require the guidance of a mental health professional. Therapy can provide a safe space to explore emotional difficulties and develop strategies to manage them effectively.

Achieving emotional balance is not a destination but a journey. It requires patience, practice, and persistence. By incorporating these strategies into daily life, individuals can take significant steps toward overcoming narcissistic behaviors and fostering a healthier, more empathetic approach to life and relation-

OVERCOMING COMPULSIVE BEHAVIORS

Compulsive behaviors, particularly compulsive lying, can be deeply ingrained habits that not only damage one's personal relationships but also hinder self-growth and self-awareness. Overcoming these behaviors requires a deep dive into self-reflection, understanding their roots, and actively employing strategies to change.

Identifying Compulsive Behaviors

The first step in addressing compulsive behaviors is recognizing their presence in your life. Compulsive lying, for instance, often stems from a need to protect oneself, project a certain image, or manipulate situations to one's advantage. It's crucial to ask yourself why you feel the need to engage in these behaviors. Is it fear of rejection, a desire for approval, or an attempt to avoid conflict? Understanding the emotional or psychological triggers can provide insight into the underlying issues that need to be addressed.

Strategies for Overcoming Compulsive Behaviors

- **Mindfulness and Self-Reflection**: Just as reflection is important in recognizing compulsive behaviors, it is equally important in addressing them. Mindfulness practices can help you become more aware of the moments when you're about to engage in compulsive behavior, allowing you the space to choose a different response.
- **Honesty with Oneself**: Begin by making a commitment to honesty, first and foremost with yourself. Acknowledge your feelings, vulnerabilities, and fears instead of hiding behind fabricated stories or actions.
- **Seek Support**: Therapeutic support can be invaluable in uncovering the reasons behind compulsive behaviors and developing healthier coping mechanisms. A therapist can provide a

non-judgmental space to explore your actions and their impacts on your life and relationships.
- **Incremental Changes**: Start with small, manageable goals. For instance, if compulsive lying is the issue, challenge yourself to be truthful in situations where you might typically lie, even if it feels uncomfortable. Reflect on these experiences, noting any anxiety or fear that arises and how you can address it healthily.
- **Develop Alternative Coping Strategies**: Identify healthier ways to deal with the emotions or situations that trigger your compulsive behaviors. This could involve assertiveness training, learning to express your needs and feelings openly, or finding constructive outlets for your emotions.
- **Accountability**: Share your goals with someone you trust and ask for their support in holding you accountable. This could mean checking in regularly about your progress or having them call out your compulsive behaviors in a compassionate way.
- **Celebrate Progress**: Recognize and celebrate your progress, no matter how small. Overcoming deep-seated behaviors takes time and effort, and every step forward is a victory.

Overcoming compulsive behaviors is not about achieving perfection but about striving for a more authentic, self-aware, and fulfilling life. It's a journey that requires patience, commitment, and a willingness to face uncomfortable truths about oneself. By continuing on this path, you not only enhance your own life but also enrich the lives of those around you with more honest and meaningful connections.

The relationship between narcissism and compulsiveness often leads individuals on a path that veers far from authenticity and honesty. Understanding this connection is crucial for anyone seeking to break free from the cyclical patterns that define compulsive behaviors within the context of narcissism.

The Connection Between Narcissism and Compulsiveness

Narcissism, at its core, involves an inflated sense of self-importance and a deep need for admiration. This can manifest in compulsive behaviors as individuals strive to maintain this grandiose self-image. Compulsive lying, for instance, might serve to embellish one's achievements or to hide perceived failures, all in an effort to sustain the illusion of superiority. Similarly, compulsive behaviors such as shopping, gambling, or even serial romantic engagements can be attempts to fill the void of unmet emotional needs, often stemming from a lack of genuine self-esteem and an inability to confront vulnerabilities.

Pathways to Authenticity and Honesty

Breaking free from the cycle of narcissism and compulsiveness requires a commitment to fostering authenticity and cultivating genuine self-awareness. This journey involves several key steps:

- **Acknowledging Vulnerability**: Embrace your vulnerabilities as part of your humanity. Recognizing and accepting your flaws and fears without judgment can pave the way for genuine self-improvement and emotional growth.
- **Cultivating Self-Compassion**: Instead of self-criticism, practice self-compassion. Understand that mistakes and failures are opportunities for learning and growth, not reflections of your worth.
- **Seeking Genuine Connections**: Strive to build relationships based on transparency and honesty. Authentic interactions with others can mirror the honesty you need to cultivate within yourself.
- **Embracing Your True Self**: Let go of the need for external validation. Your value does not lie in your accomplishments, possessions, or how others perceive you, but in your inherent worth as an individual.
- **Therapeutic Intervention**: Therapy can be a powerful tool in addressing the roots of compulsive behaviors and narcissistic tendencies. A therapist can guide you through the process of understanding and breaking these patterns, helping you to develop healthier coping mechanisms.

- **Mindful Living**: Practice mindfulness to stay present and aware of your thoughts, feelings, and actions. Mindfulness can help you recognize the onset of compulsive behaviors and choose more authentic responses.
- **Reflecting on Your Journey**: Regularly reflect on your progress. Acknowledge your successes and setbacks with compassion and understanding, viewing them as steps on your path to a more authentic self.

Beginning on a journey toward breaking the cycle of narcissism and compulsiveness to embrace authenticity and honesty is no small feat. It demands courage, dedication, and a willingness to confront uncomfortable truths about oneself. However, the reward—a life lived with integrity, genuine self-esteem, and fulfilling relationships—is immeasurably valuable. This transformative process not only reshapes your interactions with others but fundamentally alters how you perceive and engage with the world around you.

ENHANCING RELATIONSHIP DYNAMICS

Deepening emotional connections within relationships is a journey that requires patience, understanding, and a genuine desire to grow closer. This aspect of personal development is not just about enhancing our relationships but also about enriching our emotional well-being and that of those we care about. By fostering deeper emotional connections, we create a safe space for vulnerability, trust, and mutual support, which are the cornerstones of any strong relationship.

The Essence of Emotional Depth

At the heart of deepening emotional connections is the ability to truly see and understand each other beyond the surface level. This understanding goes beyond merely knowing one's likes or dislikes; it's about grasping the essence of their fears, hopes, dreams, and the experiences that have shaped them. Achieving this level of connection requires a willingness to be open and vulnerable, sharing parts of ourselves that we might usually keep hidden.

Building Blocks of a Deeper Connection

- **Empathy**: Empathy is the ability to put ourselves in someone else's shoes and feel what they are feeling. It's about listening without judgment and understanding from their perspective. When we approach our relationships with empathy, we open the door to deeper emotional connections.
- **Communication**: Honest and open communication is vital. It involves expressing our own needs and feelings clearly and listening actively to our partner's. This includes discussing not just the day-to-day matters but also the deeper issues and what we are feeling emotionally.
- **Quality Time**: Spending quality time together, engaging in activities that both enjoy, or even just being in each other's company, can strengthen the bond. It's about making the most of the moments we share and being fully present during them.
- **Support and Encouragement**: Showing support for each other's goals and dreams can profoundly deepen the emotional connection. It's about being each other's cheerleader, offering encouragement during challenging times, and celebrating successes together.
- **Respect for Individuality**: Recognizing and respecting each other's individuality is crucial. This means allowing each other the space to grow independently while growing together as a couple. It's about understanding that each partner is a complete individual outside of the relationship.

Challenges and Overcoming Them

Deepening emotional connections is not without its challenges. It requires continuous effort and isn't always straightforward. Misunderstandings, life stresses, and past traumas can act as barriers. However, these challenges can be through patience, perseverance, and a commitment to working through issues together.

Enhancing the dynamics of our relationships by deepening emotional connections is a testament to the human capacity for growth and change. It not only improves our relationships but also contributes significantly to our journey of self-improvement. As we progress on this path, let us cherish the deep connections we foster, for they are the threads that weave the fabric of our lives into a richer tapestry.

In the next sections, we will explore further strategies for personal development, building upon the foundation of self-reflection and the deepening of our relationships. Together, we continue on this journey of transformation, ready to face whatever comes next with resilience, empathy, and an unwavering commitment to growth.

Strategies for long-term healthy relationship maintenance

Maintaining long-term relationships, whether they be romantic, familial, or platonic, requires continuous effort, commitment, and a willingness to adapt and grow together. The essence of sustaining these relationships lies not just in the joyous moments but in navigating the challenges and changes that inevitably come over time. Here, we explore strategies that can help in fostering enduring bonds.

The Foundation of Trust and Communication

The bedrock of any lasting relationship is trust, nurtured through open and honest communication. It's about creating an environment where both parties feel safe to express their thoughts, feelings, and vulnerabilities without fear of judgment. This entails active listening, where we not only hear but truly understand what the other person is saying. Regular, heartfelt conversations about each other's needs, expectations, and concerns help in reinforcing this trust and ensuring both parties are on the same page.

Embracing Change and Growth

As individuals, we are constantly evolving, and so are our relationships. Embracing change rather than resisting it is key to sustaining long-term bonds. This means being supportive of each other's personal growth and changes in aspirations or beliefs. It's about growing together, not apart, and finding new ways to connect and share experiences as you both evolve.

Cultivating Shared Values and Goals

While it's essential to celebrate individuality, having shared values and goals can significantly strengthen a relationship. These commonalities become the threads that hold the fabric of the relationship together, especially during challenging times. Whether it's family values, life goals, or simply shared interests, these elements can foster a deeper sense of unity and purpose.

Cultivating Intimacy and Affection

Intimacy and affection are vital components of a robust relationship, going beyond physical closeness to include emotional and intellectual intimacy. It's about maintaining a connection that feels both comforting and exhilarating. Small gestures of love, appreciation, and gratitude contribute significantly to this aspect, reminding both parties of their bond and mutual affection.

Resolving Conflicts with Respect and Love

Conflict is an inevitable part of any relationship, but it's the approach to resolution that determines the impact on the relationship's longevity. Addressing disagreements with respect, empathy, and a willingness to understand the other person's perspective can turn conflicts into opportunities for growth. It's about finding solutions that respect both parties' needs and feelings, ensuring that the relationship becomes stronger through the resolution process.

Continuously Investing in the Relationship

Like any long-term project, relationships require continuous investment of time, effort, and emotional energy. This could mean setting aside quality time together, engaging in shared hobbies, or simply checking in with each other regularly. The key is to remain actively engaged in the relationship, showing commitment and care through both actions and words.

Long-term relationship maintenance is a dynamic process that adapts as life changes. By employing these strategies, individuals can nurture their relationships, ensuring they thrive over the years. The journey of sustaining deep connections is both challenging and rewarding, offering endless opportunities for growth, joy, and fulfillment. As we move forward, let us cherish the beauty of enduring relationships, recognizing them as the pillars of our personal development journey.

. . .

Intimacy and closeness, the core elements that bind any relationship, are as complex as they are essential. They are the quiet yet powerful forces that draw individuals together, creating a bond that is both vulnerable and strong. As we dive into enhancing relationship dynamics, understanding and navigating the intricacies of intimacy and closeness become paramount. Furthermore, mutual respect and understanding serve as the bedrock of these deep connections.

The Essence of Intimacy and Closeness

Intimacy transcends the physical, encompassing emotional, intellectual, and sometimes spiritual connections that foster a deep sense of closeness between individuals. It involves a willingness to share one's true self, including hopes, fears, and dreams, with another person. This sharing, in turn, cultivates a closeness that can weather the storms of life, making the relationship resilient and adaptable.

Navigating intimacy involves constant communication and the courage to be vulnerable. It's about creating a safe space where each person feels seen, heard, and valued. This process is dynamic, evolving as each individual grows. Thus, maintaining intimacy requires a commitment to continuous engagement and rediscovery of each other.

The Role of Mutual Respect and Understanding

Mutual respect and understanding are the cornerstones of any healthy relationship. Respect involves recognizing and valuing the other person's boundaries, feelings, and needs. It means appreciating the individuality of the other and supporting their growth and aspirations.

Understanding, on the other hand, requires empathy and active listening. It's about trying to see the world from your partner's perspective, feeling with them, and acknowledging their emotions without judgment. This understanding fosters a deeper emotional connection, making it easier to challenge and conflict together.

Strategies for Enhancing Intimacy and Closeness

- **Regular Check-ins**: Establish a routine of checking in with each other, discussing your feelings, experiences, and needs. This

practice keeps the lines of communication open and strengthens emotional intimacy.
- **Shared Experiences**: Engage in activities that both enjoy, creating new memories and shared experiences. These can range from travel to engaging in a shared hobby, contributing to a reservoir of joy and closeness.
- **Cultivate Empathy**: Actively work on understanding and empathizing with your partner. Try to put yourself in their shoes, especially during disagreements, to foster understanding and resolution.
- **Appreciate the Small Things**: Express gratitude for the little things your partner does. Small acts of kindness and appreciation can significantly impact the warmth and closeness in a relationship.
- **Seek Growth Together**: Encourage and support each other in personal growth and learning. Taking courses together, exploring new interests, or setting joint goals can be incredibly bonding.

Navigating the complexities of intimacy and closeness, underpinned by mutual respect and understanding, is a journey of constant learning and adaptation. It's about being present, empathetic, and committed to the growth of the relationship. As we venture into these depths, we not only enhance our relationships but also discover more about our capacities for love, understanding, and connection. The rewards of this journey are profound, leading to relationships that are deeply fulfilling and resilient in the face of life's challenges.

CHAPTER 8
RELAPSE PREVENTION AND CONTINUOUS IMPROVEMENT

IDENTIFYING SIGNS OF RELAPSE

In the journey of overcoming narcissism, relapse is a real possibility, just as it is in the process of overcoming any deeply ingrained behavior. Recognizing the early warning signs of slipping back into narcissistic patterns is crucial for sustaining long-term change. Moreover, developing strategies for addressing and preventing relapse can help maintain the progress you've made on this transformative path.

Early Warning Signs of Relapse into Narcissism

- **Increased Sensitivity to Criticism**: Finding yourself increasingly defensive or upset in response to feedback could indicate a slip back into narcissistic tendencies.
- **Feeling Superior or Entitled**: Catching yourself expecting special treatment or believing you're superior to others is a red flag.
- **Manipulative Behaviors**: Reverting to manipulation to get your way or to influence others' perceptions can be a sign of relapse.

- **Lack of Empathy**: Noticing a decrease in your ability to empathize with others or a disinterest in their feelings and experiences.
- **Seeking Excessive Admiration**: Increasingly seeking validation and admiration from others, especially in superficial ways, indicates a potential backslide.

Strategies for Addressing and Preventing Relapse

- **Self-awareness Practice**: Continue to cultivate self-awareness through reflection and mindfulness. Acknowledging these signs in yourself is the first step to addressing them.
- **Seek Feedback**: Maintain open lines of communication with trusted friends or family who can help you see when you might be slipping into old patterns. Feedback is invaluable for self-correction.
- **Engage in Therapy**: Regular sessions with a therapist, especially one familiar with narcissistic behavior, can provide support and strategies for managing relapse indicators.
- **Practice Empathy**: Deliberately practicing empathy can help counteract narcissistic tendencies. Try to understand others' perspectives and feelings without judgment.
- **Set Healthy Boundaries**: Establishing and maintaining healthy boundaries with yourself and others can prevent the resurgence of manipulative behaviors.
- **Journaling**: Keep a journal to track your thoughts, feelings, and behaviors. This can help you identify patterns and triggers that may lead to relapse.
- **Commit to Continuous Learning**: Stay engaged with books, workshops, and groups focused on emotional growth and narcissism recovery. Ongoing education can reinforce your commitment to change.

Preventing relapse into narcissism is an ongoing process that requires vigilance, commitment, and a willingness to continuously reflect and adjust one's behavior. By recognizing the early signs of relapse and employing strategies to address them, individuals can maintain the progress they've made towards becoming more empathetic, self-aware, and relationally healthy. Remember, transformation is a journey, not a destination, and each step forward, no matter how small, is a victory in itself.

Self-awareness is the cornerstone of preventing a relapse into narcissistic behaviors. It's the skill that allows us to recognize the difference between being in control of our actions and being controlled by our impulses. Cultivating self-awareness is an ongoing process, requiring commitment and honesty with oneself. The importance of this trait cannot be overstated in the context of relapse prevention, as it empowers individuals to identify and address the early signs of slipping back into unhealthy patterns.

The Importance of Self-Awareness in Relapse Prevention

Self-awareness facilitates a deep understanding of one's emotions, thoughts, and behaviors, enabling the recognition of narcissistic tendencies as they arise. It's about acknowledging vulnerabilities and triggers without judgment, allowing for a proactive approach to managing them. This self-knowledge serves as a foundation for personal growth and resilience, essential for navigating the complexities of changing deep-seated patterns.

CONCLUSION AND REFLECTIONS

Well, folks, we've reached the end of our journey together. From recognizing those tricky narcissistic behaviors in ourselves to learning how to build empathy, manage anger, and set healthy boundaries, what a ride it's been! We've navigated the often bumpy road of self-awareness, tackled the challenge of creating healthier relationships, and even started planting the seeds for a more connected and fulfilling life.

Let's not forget the key lessons we've picked up along the way: Understanding narcissism isn't about labeling yourself but about recognizing behaviors and their impact on others. Developing empathy and self-awareness takes time and practice, but the payoff is stronger, healthier relationships. Setting boundaries isn't about pushing people away; it's about creating a safe space for everyone involved. And managing anger and control issues is crucial for maintaining those meaningful connections.

Staying committed to personal growth isn't a one-time sprint; it's more like an ongoing adventure that never ends. It demands our attention, effort, and most importantly, consistency. Keep working on self-awareness, adjust your strategies as life throws new challenges your way, and never stop striving to build empathy and improve your relationships.

Now, consider this book not as the final chapter but as the beginning of your journey towards emotional and relational well-being. There's a whole world of personal growth out there waiting for you. Dive into new resources, challenge yourself with fresh goals, and keep expanding your understanding. The path to becoming a more empathetic and self-aware individual is yours to explore.

So, what's your next move? Pick just one thing from our time together and put it into action today. Whether it's practicing a new empathy exercise, setting a healthy boundary, or simply reflecting on your interactions, start somewhere. Every big change begins with a single, often small, step.

Reflecting on my own journey, from struggling with narcissistic behaviors to building stronger, more meaningful relationships, I've stumbled, faced tough realizations, but also grown tremendously. If this guy can find his way, so can you. Your future self will thank you, trust me.

Lastly, I want to shout a massive thank you from the rooftops (or, well, from this page). Thank you for trusting me with your time, for being open to change, and for taking these brave steps towards improving your relationships and understanding yourself better. If you've found a spark of inspiration or a helpful nudge within these pages, consider passing the baton to a friend or family member. After all, the best journeys are those we share.

Here's to our continued journey towards personal growth, to the highs, the lows, and every moment in between. Keep striving, my friends.

Your fellow journeyer in personal growth,

Max Reed

FREE GIFT FOR MY READERS

Download 6 bonuses: a daily journal, an ebook, two audiobooks, video, 60+ exercises with 60-day plan.

BONUS: THE POWER OF MINDFULNESS AND MEDITATION

In our journey towards self-improvement, mindfulness and meditation emerge as powerful practices that can significantly impact our ability to understand and manage narcissistic tendencies. By fostering a deep sense of present-moment awareness and cultivating inner peace, these practices enable us to navigate the complexities of our thoughts and emotions with grace and empathy.

Mindfulness: A Path to Presence

Mindfulness is the practice of being fully engaged in the present moment, without judgment or distraction. It's about noticing your thoughts, feelings, bodily sensations, and the surrounding environment with an attitude of curiosity and kindness.

Daily Mindfulness Practices:

- Mindful Breathing: Spend a few minutes each day focusing solely on your breath. Notice the sensation of air entering and leaving your nostrils, and the rise and fall of your chest.
- Mindful Eating: Engage all your senses when eating. Notice the colors, textures, flavors, and smells of your food. Chew slowly and savor each bite.

- Mindful Walking: Take a walk and pay attention to each step. Notice the feel of the ground under your feet, the air on your skin, and the sounds around you.

Meditation: Cultivating Inner Peace

Meditation is the practice of turning your attention inward, fostering a state of deep relaxation and heightened awareness. Regular meditation can help reduce stress, improve emotional balance, and increase empathy and understanding towards oneself and others.

Simple Meditation Techniques:

- Guided Meditation: Use a guided meditation app or audio track. Follow the voice and instructions to focus your mind and enter a state of relaxation.
- Mantra Meditation: Repeat a calming word or phrase, such as "peace" or "let go," either silently or aloud, to help focus your thoughts.
- Visualization: Picture a serene environment or situation. Immerse yourself in the details and sensations of this peaceful place to calm your mind.

Integrating Mindfulness and Meditation into Your Life

- Set aside a specific time each day for your practice, even if it's just for five minutes.
- Create a comfortable space where you won't be interrupted.
- Be patient and kind to yourself. Mindfulness and meditation are skills that develop over time.
- Reflect on your progress. Keep a journal of your experiences and any changes you notice in your thoughts, feelings, and behaviors.

THE TRANSFORMATIVE POWER

Mindfulness and meditation can transform the way we relate to ourselves and the world around us. By practicing these disciplines, we learn to approach life with a greater sense of calm, clarity, and compassion. These practices encourage us to pause before reacting, allowing us to choose responses that align with our values and foster healthier relationships. As a bonus to your journey of overcoming narcissism, embracing mindfulness and meditation can be a gateway to a more balanced, empathetic, and connected life.

Incorporating a case story to illustrate the transformative power of mindfulness and meditation, let's explore the journey of Michael, a man whose life was radically changed by these practices.

Case Story: Michael's Transformation

Michael, a 42-year-old executive, had achieved great success in his career but felt his personal life was falling apart. His aggressive leadership style, once a source of pride, had strained his relationships and shortened his temper. He often felt isolated and misunderstood, wondering if there was a better way to live and lead.

One day, after a particularly tense board meeting, Michael stumbled upon an article about mindfulness in a business magazine. Although he was skeptical, the idea intrigued him. Could mindfulness help him manage his volatility and improve his life? He decided to give it a try, hoping for a change. Michael began with simple breathing exercises. Every morning, before starting his busy day, he would sit quietly and focus on his breath. At first, it seemed too simple to be effective, but he soon noticed a shift. He started to become more aware of the present moment and felt calmer. Encouraged by these small changes, Michael added meditation to his routine. Each evening, he spent 15 minutes in silence, using guided meditations to help him explore his inner thoughts and feelings. This practice became a sanctuary for him, a place where he could confront his emotions without the stress of his daily responsibilities.

How did these practices affect Michael's life? Let's look at the changes he experienced:

- At Work: Michael noticed a big difference in how he led his team. He became more patient and listened actively to his colleagues. His decisions were still confident, but now he also considered their impact on people and relationships. His team responded positively, showing more engagement and creativity.
- In Personal Relationships: Michael's family and friends saw a change in him too. He was no longer quick to anger or dismissive. Instead, he showed genuine interest in their lives, which helped him build deeper connections and understanding with those around him.
- Self-Perception: Most importantly, Michael's view of himself began to change. He realized his worth wasn't just in his achievements but also in his ability to connect, understand, and be present with others. He started to see himself as a more empathetic and balanced person.

Michael's journey shows how powerful mindfulness and meditation can be. These practices helped him transform from a reactive and isolated leader into one characterized by empathy, presence, and a deep sense of inner peace. His story reminds us that even small steps toward mindfulness can lead to significant changes in our lives.As you reflect on Michael's story, think about your own life. Are there areas where you feel isolated or reactive? Could mindfulness help you find a different path? Remember, change doesn't happen overnight, but with patience and practice, you too can experience the profound impact of mindfulness.

Reflecting on the Case

Michael's journey underscores a vital message: transformation begins within. By turning our attention inward, we unlock the potential for profound change in how we relate to ourselves and the world around us. Mindfulness and meditation are not merely practices but pathways to becoming more authentically ourselves, fostering relationships and interactions characterized by depth, understanding, and respect.

KEEPING THE JOURNEY GOING

Now that you've learned how to build healthier relationships and overcome narcissistic behaviors, it's time to share what you've discovered with others who might need the same help.

By leaving your honest opinion of this book on Amazon, you can guide other readers to the information they're searching for. Your review could be the encouragement they need to start their own journey.

Thank you for your help. This journey toward change and growth stays alive when we share what we've learned—and you're helping me do just that.

Just scan the QR code below to leave your review:

AUTHOR'S NOTE

Hey there,

I just wanted to take a moment to say a heartfelt thank you for picking up this book and joining me on this journey. Writing "How to Stop Being a Narcissist" has been a labor of love, filled with personal reflections, hard-won insights, and a genuine desire to help others navigate the complex world of narcissistic behaviors and relationships.

This book isn't just about sharing what I've learned; it's about connecting with you, the reader, and offering a supportive hand as you work towards positive change. I hope you've found the tools, strategies, and encouragement you need to start making meaningful improvements in your life and relationships.

Remember, transformation doesn't happen overnight. It's a journey filled with ups and downs, but every step you take towards self-awareness and empathy is a step in the right direction. Keep going, stay committed, and know that you're not alone on this path.

Thank you for allowing me to be a part of your journey. Here's to a brighter, more empathetic future!

Warmly,
Max Reed

REFERENCES

Furnham, A., & Cuppello, S. (2024). Correlates of the Dark Tetrad. *Acta psychologica*, *245*, 104222. Advance online publication. https://doi.org/10.1016/j.actpsy.2024.104222

Manunta, E., Becker, M., Vignoles, V. L., Bertin, P., Crapolicchio, E., Contreras, C., Gavreliuc, A., González, R., Manzi, C., Salanova, T., & Easterbrook, M. J. (2024). Populism, Economic Distress, Cultural Backlash, and Identity Threat: Integrating Patterns and Testing Cross-National Validity. *Personality & social psychology bulletin*, 1461672241231727. Advance online publication. https://doi.org/10.1177/01461672241231727

Pryor, J. B., Stutterheim, S. E., & Lemmens, L. H. J. M. (2024). The relationships of sexually harassing behaviors to organizational context factors and working men's dark personality traits. *Aggressive behavior*, *50*(2), e22142. https://doi.org/10.1002/ab.22142

Sprio, V., Mirra, L., Madeddu, F., Lopez-Castroman, J., Blasco-Fontecilla, H., Di Pierro, R., & Calati, R. (2024). Can clinical and subclinical forms of narcissism be considered risk factors for suicide-related outcomes? A systematic review. *Journal of psychiatric research*, *172*, 307–333. https://doi.org/10.1016/j.jpsychires.2024.02.017

Spytska L. (2024). Narcissistic Trauma: Main Characteristics and Life Impact. *The Journal of nervous and mental disease*, 10.1097/NMD.0000000000001760. Advance online publication. https://doi.org/10.1097/NMD.0000000000001760

Schokkenbroek, J. M., Hauspie, T., Ponnet, K., & Hardyns, W. (2024). Malevolent Monitoring: Dark Triad Traits, Cyber Dating Abuse, and the Instrumental Role of Self-Control. *Journal of interpersonal violence*, 8862605241233263. Advance online publication. https://doi.org/10.1177/08862605241233263

Oliver, E., Coates, A., Bennett, J. M., & Willis, M. L. (2023). Narcissism and Intimate Partner Violence: A Systematic Review and Meta-Analysis. *Trauma, violence & abuse*, 15248380231196115. Advance online publication. https://doi.org/10.1177/15248380231196115

Klein, J. P., Schaich, A., & Furukawa, T. A. (2023). How should narcissism be treated best?. *The lancet. Psychiatry*, *10*(12), 914–916. https://doi.org/10.1016/S2215-0366(23)00307-3

Czarna, A. Z., Mauersberger, H., Kastendieck, T., Zdunek, R. R., Sedikides, C., & Hess, U. (2023). Narcissism predicts noise perception but not signal decoding in emotion. *Scientific reports*, *13*(1), 14457. https://doi.org/10.1038/s41598-023-41792-0

Adekeye A. P. (2023). The veil of intention: Narcissism and leadership. *Industrial psychiatry journal*, *32*(2), 462–463. https://doi.org/10.4103/ipj.ipj_54_23

Wallace, H. M., Carrillo, A., & Kelley, J. (2024). Perceptions of narcissism in college professors. *The Journal of social psychology*, *164*(2), 169–186. https://doi.org/10.1080/00224545.2022.2050167

Rawn, K. P., Keller, P. S., & Widiger, T. A. (2023). Parent Grandiose Narcissism and Child Socio-

Emotional Well Being: The Role of Parenting. *Psychological reports*, 332941231208900. Advance online publication. https://doi.org/10.1177/00332941231208900

Gao, S., Yu, D., Assink, M., Chan, K. L., Zhang, L., & Meng, X. (2024). The Association Between Child Maltreatment and Pathological Narcissism: A Three-Level Meta-Analytic Review. *Trauma, violence & abuse*, 25(1), 275–290. https://doi.org/10.1177/15248380221147559

Bağatarhan, T., Siyez, D. M., & Vazsonyi, A. T. (2023). The Importance of Narcissism and Impulsivity for Bullying and Cyberbullying Perpetration. *Violence and victims*, 38(6), 879–896. https://doi.org/10.1891/VV-2022-0149

Akıncı, İ., & Gençöz, T. (2023). How Do Grandiose and Vulnerable Narcissism Relate to Psychological Symptoms?: The Role of Emotions. *Psychological reports*, 332941231197167. Advance online publication. https://doi.org/10.1177/00332941231197167

Vecchione, M., Vacca, M., Dentale, F., Spagnolo, G., Lombardo, C., Geukes, K., & Back, M. D. (2023). Prospective associations between grandiose narcissism and perfectionism: A longitudinal study in adolescence. *The British journal of developmental psychology*, 41(2), 172–186. https://doi.org/10.1111/bjdp.12441

Harhoff, N., Reinhardt, N., Reinhard, M. A., & Mayer, M. (2023). Agentic and communal narcissism in predicting different types of lies in romantic relationships. *Frontiers in psychology*, 14, 1146732. https://doi.org/10.3389/fpsyg.2023.1146732

Sivanathan, D., Bizumic, B., Li, W., & Chen, J. (2023). The Unified Narcissism Scale-Revised: Expanding Measurement and Understanding of Narcissism Across Cultures. *Assessment*, 10731911231191435. Advance online publication. https://doi.org/10.1177/10731911231191435

Made in United States
Troutdale, OR
03/12/2025